Ubuntu on a Dime
The Path to Low-Cost Computing

■ ■ ■

James Floyd Kelly

Apress®

Ubuntu on a Dime: The Path to Low-Cost Computing

Copyright © 2009 by James Floyd Kelly

ISBN-13 (pbk): 978-1-4302-1972-9

ISBN-13 (electronic): 978-1-4302-1973-6

Printed and bound in the United States of America 9 8 7 6 5 4 3 2 1

Lead Editor: Frank Pohlmann, Michelle Lowman
Technical Reviewer: Harrison Sia
Editorial Board: Clay Andres, Steve Anglin, Mark Beckner, Ewan Buckingham, Tony Campbell,
    Gary Cornell, Jonathan Gennick, Michelle Lowman, Matthew Moodie, Jeffrey Pepper, Frank Pohlmann,
    Ben Renow-Clarke, Dominic Shakeshaft, Matt Wade, Tom Welsh
Project Manager: Denise Santoro Lincoln
Copy Editor: Nancy Sixsmith
Associate Production Director: Kari Brooks-Copony
Production Editor: Ellie Fountain
Compositor: Regina Rexrode
Proofreader: Kim Burton
Indexer: Becky Hornyak
Artist: Kinetic Publishing Services, LLC
Cover Designer: Kurt Krames
Manufacturing Director: Tom Debolski

Distributed to the book trade worldwide by Springer-Verlag New York, Inc., 233 Spring Street, 6th Floor, New York, NY 10013. Phone 1-800-SPRINGER, fax 201-348-4505, e-mail orders-ny@springer-sbm.com, or visit http://www.springeronline.com.

For information on translations, please contact Apress directly at 2855 Telegraph Avenue, Suite 600, Berkeley, CA 94705. Phone 510-549-5930, fax 510-549-5939, e-mail info@apress.com, or visit http://www.apress.com.

Apress and friends of ED books may be purchased in bulk for academic, corporate, or promotional use. eBook versions and licenses are also available for most titles. For more information, reference our Special Bulk Sales–eBook Licensing web page at http://www.apress.com/info/bulksales.

For my friend, Tony (http://www.friendsoftony.org)

Contents at a Glance

Contents

About the Author

JAMES FLOYD KELLY is a freelance writer who lives in Atlanta, Georgia. He has degrees in both English and industrial engineering because he couldn't decide between majoring in liberal arts or math and science. Fortunately, technical writing uses both sides of the brain, and James has been able to write on a variety of topics, including LEGO robotics, free software, netbooks, and building a homemade CNC machine. James is the editor in chief of the number one LEGO NXT Robotics blog, The NXT Step (http://www.thenxtstep.com). When not writing, he and his wife enjoy watching their little boy discover all kinds of new and exciting things about the world.

About the Technical Reviewer

 **HARRISON SIA** has more than 12 years of software engineering experience in the design, development, testing, and maintenance of various applications for Windows and Unix systems (primarily for telecommunication systems). He spends his free time playing online games and playing around with his Ubuntu desktop system.

Acknowledgments

I'm one of those people who are always hoping that their skills are improving instead of rusting. When it comes to my books, I have a great little collection of people at Apress who have made certain that my writing skills are improving with every new title. Any positive feedback you have for the book must be shared with Dominic Shakeshaft, Frank Pohlmann, Michelle Lowman, Denise Santoro Lincoln, Harrison Sia, Ellie Fountain, and Nancy Sixsmith. My *Ubuntu on a Dime* team kept this book on target and helped me track down all those pesky technical, spelling, and grammar errors that many authors won't admit ever happen. I'm not one of them. I must yell loudly and proudly a huge "Thank you!" to all of them for the great job they did in helping my book shine.

I now understand why so many authors thank their spouses for support during the writing of a book. Writing isn't always a 9-to-5 job for me; it's an up and down, when-the-muse-strikes ordeal for me. Unfortunately, my wife is often scratching her head and wondering why all of a sudden I have to be typing in my office late at night or rising with the chickens to get working on a chapter. Thank you, Ashley, for your understanding and patience. The nomination for Wife of the Year is in the mail.

I have a home office that is very quiet at times. As someone who worked in an office environment for the first four years after graduating from college, I sometimes need some background noise and hustle and bustle. When I have to get out of the house and actually work, I head down to my favorite hangout and "second office," Atlanta Bread Company, which has free WiFi, free refills, and a staff who recognizes me and usually has my chocolate chip cookie ready before I make it to the cash register. The music is quiet, the temperature is just right, and the booths let me spread out and get to work. A huge thanks to ABC for a great place "to get some writin' done."

Introduction

I will never—*never!*—purchase an expensive computer again. It's getting almost as bad as purchasing a new car. You drive it off the lot and it immediately drops 10 percent or more in value. And when you buy new hardware and software, one week later the same computer is $200 cheaper or—even worse—a newer model with more and better hardware is out and is $300 cheaper! Argh!

I go through computers fast in my line of work. I wear out a laptop in about two years. My desktop computer frequently has half a dozen or more operating system reinstalls in a year so that I can take screenshots of the installation, test software compatibility, and more. I'm always pulling out some piece of hardware to pop in a newer piece of hardware. (I've been known to drop a piece of sensitive hardware—another trip to the computer store!) Costs start to add up.

In late 2008, my test computer (nicknamed FrankenPC) died. The autopsy I performed was inconclusive; I think the little desktop just lost the will to compute: RIP, FrankenPC.

I found myself sitting down and listing the things I wanted in a basic little desktop test PC:

- I wanted to keep the cost down. Under $250 would be great, but was it realistic?

- I needed to be able to access the Internet (a realistic expectation these days, right?).

- It would be one of three computers that I would use for e-mail: laptop, netbook, and desktop.

- I needed some basic apps such as a word processor, spreadsheet, and such to run on it.

- I planned to use it to store my large music collection (more than 2,000 songs).

- I needed it to have a CD/DVD writer so I could back up my data to disc (and make music CDs).

Not a whole lot to ask for, in my opinion. I went online and started my search with the usual suspects: Dell, HP, and so on. But what I found was that the low-end computers they were selling were still being packed with the latest/greatest hardware and a lot of software that I didn't really want or need. Why couldn't I tell them the exact processor and amount of memory I needed as well as the speeds and specifications of the other hardware I wanted? I asked a friend who keeps up on all the computer technology much more than I do. And (here's where the story gets interesting!) he dared me to build my own computer and satisfy my requirements including the low price. A dare? Is he kidding? Aren't we both out of school?

After much deliberation and soul searching, I came to one simple conclusion: I would accept his challenge and prove to all our colleagues that an inexpensive yet useful computer is easy to build and install with loads of free software.

Oh, and because I was writing another book for Apress at the time, I politely inquired whether they might be interested in a book about building a cheap, no-frills computer. They were interested. The story ends with the book you're holding in your hands.

It was a fun experience. There was the research required to keep my costs low—I found a free operating system that I can't wait to introduce to you. There were the numerous visits to my computer store to shop for the ideal hardware components (I kept my receipts and have provided you with the exact shopping list in Appendix A). There was the actual building of my new computer: I wrote down everything and photographed all my steps so you can follow along and build your own. And finally there was the installation of the free operating system and testing of various applications (all free!) to make sure that my new computer worked.

My new computer is sitting beside my desk and I use it daily; I check my e-mail, back up my chapters as I write them, and listen to music and browse the Internet for my next book idea. The final price? Two hundred dollars! You'll have to keep reading to find out exactly what I purchased and how it all came together, but I can promise you that building a similar PC is within your grasp. For me, the days of spending huge amounts of money on the latest PC are over; when I need a new desktop computer, I'll build it myself, thank you very much.

Are you ready to do the same thing? Have you decided that a new computer would be nice? How about a new computer that has inside what you want at the price you decided on? If this sounds great to you, welcome to Ubuntu on a Dime. You'll have fun, save some money, learn a new skill, and end up with a whiz-bang new PC to brag about. Don't believe me? Keep reading. I dare you.

CHAPTER 1

■ ■ ■

The Hardware

First, the good news: every piece of software you'll learn about in this book, including the Ubuntu operating system, is 100 percent free—free to download, free to install, and free to use. I might as well go ahead and say that the software is also free to uninstall, free to love or hate, free to complain about, and, of course, free to rave about to your friends and family.

And now the bad news: unless a major breakthrough in direct-to-brain downloading has occurred as you read this, that 100 percent free operating system and software will need a home. And that means a computer—a whirring, beeping, plugged-in personal computer (PC) that contains a few basic components that are absolutely required for you to download, store, and use the previously mentioned software.

But there's more good news. It is no longer mandatory that you spend a bundle of money to be able to install an operating system and all the software you know you'll want to use. Let me explain.

In early 2007, Microsoft introduced its latest operating system, Vista, to the world. It then promptly informed everyone that running the operating system properly would require some hefty computer hardware requirements: more hard drive space than any previous operating system, more memory, and a much faster processor. And those requirements were the minimum just to run Vista; other limits existed. For example, if you wanted to have all the fancy new graphics features, you'd have to invest in a faster (and more expensive) video card. It wasn't uncommon to find users spending $500 or more on hardware upgrades. And in many instances a completely new computer would need to be purchased if the user wanted to run Vista; older computers simply didn't meet the requirements.

Have you had enough? Are you tired of spending dollar after dollar chasing the dream of the "perfect PC?" Are you looking for an inexpensive but scalable (upgradeable) computer that can provide you with basic services such as e-mail, word processing, and Internet browsing? And don't forget other features, such as Internet messaging, VOIP (using your Internet connection to make phone calls), photo editing, and games. You shouldn't have to skimp on any services or features. Does this sound like a computer you'd enjoy owning and using?

If so, today's your lucky day. Because I'll show you how easy it is to put together your own computer using inexpensive components. And because you won't be spending any money on software, you'll have the option to put some (or all) of those savings into your new computer. You might splurge and buy a bigger LCD panel (or a second LCD for multiple-monitor usage!) or add some more memory so you can run more applications at once. Or you can spend the bare minimum on hardware, keeping your expenditures low without skimping on software and services. (And if you want to get some more life out of your existing computer, I'll explain how you can possibly give it a second life by installing Ubuntu to save even more money!)

This chapter is all about the types of hardware you'll need to run Ubuntu as well as a good collection of free software such as a word processor, calendar, e-mail application, and more. I gave this computer the nickname *U-PC* for purposes of talking about it throughout the remainder of the book's chapters. So, let's get started building the U-PC.

Basic Components

You've probably heard the phrase, "Your mileage may vary," and it's no truer than when dealing with different computer hardware settings running Ubuntu (or any operating system). But when it comes to the Ubuntu operating system versus the Windows operating system, there is one large difference in hardware requirements: Ubuntu requires substantially less "oomph" when it comes to the basic components you need inside your computer. By this, I mean you don't need the fastest processor, a huge amount of RAM memory, or even a large capacity hard drive.

The recommended Ubuntu hardware consists of the following:

- 700MHz x86 processor

- 384MB system memory (RAM)

- 8GB disk space

- Graphics card capable of 1024x768 resolution

- Sound card

- Network or Internet connection

Note that you don't need an Intel 3GHz (gigahertz) Core 2 Duo processor with 2GB (gigabytes) of RAM and 500GB hard drive to install the Vista Ultimate operating system. You can install the latest version of Ubuntu on cutting-edge hardware found in a computer from 2000. Back in 2000, a good computer might typically come with a 60GB hard drive, 512MB or 1GB of RAM memory, and a Pentium 4 processor; as well as a built-in network card, video, and sound on the motherboard. Surprised?

This means that it's possible for you to install Ubuntu on your current computer (or an older one you've packed away and hidden in a closet somewhere). Ubuntu doesn't put a lot of demand on hardware, so you can use your current computer or build your own, but avoid the latest bleeding-edge technology (that also comes with a bleeding-edge price).

Not convinced? Okay, here's where I put my money where my mouth is and show you just how easy it is to build a computer that will run Ubuntu and hundreds more applications for very little money. What's even better is that I'm 99.9 percent certain that in five years this computer will most likely run the latest version of Ubuntu. Can you say that about your current computer and, say, Windows 2014 Home Edition?

In the introduction of this book, I mentioned that I wanted to build a basic computer that would satisfy a number of requirements:

- It must cost me less than $250.00.

- It must allow me to access the Internet.

- It must also let me access my e-mail, either via the Internet or stored on my hard drive.

- It must provide me with basic productivity features: word processor, spreadsheet, and slideshow-creation software.

- It must allow me to play music and create my own CDs or DVDs.

This list helps define the hardware I need to purchase to build my U-PC. What hardware? Well, even if you're not familiar with the inner workings of your computer, I'll make this as simple as I can for you.

Case

All computers require a case to hold the hardware; inside that case must be a power supply that plugs into the wall and provides power to all the hardware that will be added inside the case.

Tip Cases come in various shapes and sizes. You've probably seen desktop models in which the computer case sits on top of the desk and usually under the monitor or LCD panel. Tower cases are usually found sitting on the floor; they can be short or tall. There are also all sorts of odd shapes, colors, and materials available for cases.

Inside the case you'll always find a motherboard (MB) and a processor. A *motherboard* can look intimidating (see Figure 1-15 later in the chapter), but it's simply a component that allows all the PC hardware to communicate. Think of it as Grand Central Station, in which all your hardware must come together—and work together—to run the operating system and applications that you install. One nice feature of most MBs is that they also can provide sound and video and network connectivity. So you can see words and pictures on the screen, hear music and any beeps your computer might make, and get connected to the Internet. (Sound, video, and network connectivity can also be provided by separate hardware called *peripherals* that plug into the MB, but they typically cost more money because they sometimes provide more features.)

Memory and Hard Drive

All computers must have memory (also called *RAM memory*) and a *hard drive* added to store information and work with it. There are better books out there on how computer hardware components work, but just know that a computer hard drive retains all the information stored on it when the power is turned off; the RAM memory can hold information when the computer is powered and it provides that information to the processor (and you) faster than the hard drive can do.

CD/DVD Drive

I also need a CD or DVD drive (or combination of the two) to install any software that comes on CD or DVD discs. And if I want to create my own CD/DVD discs by writing information to them (also called *burning*), I need my drive to be the read/write (R-W) type.

Tip The standard CD or DVD drive can only read discs, not write data or music. If you want to back up your files to a disc or create your own music CDs, you'll need a drive that can write data to discs. Look for a drive labeled as RW. To add to the confusion, CD and DVD drives can be found in CD+RW, DVD+RW, CD-RW, and CD-RW. The +/- symbols indicate a specific way that data is written to a disc by the drive and the type of disc that goes in it. Purchase blank discs that match the drive type; for example, buy DVD-RW discs if you have purchased a DVD-RW drive. Not sure which to buy? I recommend a CD/DVD combo unit that writes in all formats; they are available! With this combo you can create music CDs (to play in your car, for example) as well as back up your data to DVDs that can hold much more data than a CD.

Buying the Necessities

Add to this mix a handful of cables to connect everything together (which I'll cover in more detail later), and this is the list of parts I need to purchase for my bare-bones U-PC:

- Computer case
- Motherboard (with built-in video, sound, and network connectivity)
- CD/DVD-RW (read/write)
- Processor (AMD or Intel brands are perfectly suitable for Ubuntu)
- RAM memory
- Hard drive

Not a long list, is it? And what's so great about buying hardware these days is that the stuff is so compatible—almost all components have standard sizes and shapes that will fit perfectly inside specific locations in the computer case. Memory chips have their own place on the MB where they fit; and it's the same with a hard drive and even the MB. There are always exceptions, however. For example, processors come in different sizes and shapes, and you must make certain to buy a MB that will accept a certain type of processor; the place where the processor is inserted is called a *socket*. (My recommendation is to always decide on the processor you want to purchase first—it might very well be the most expensive part found in the case—and then purchase the MB that is compatible.)

■Tip When in doubt, always ask. Ask your salesperson if you're buying the components locally. If you're ordering online, call and ask questions before placing your order. Most reliable companies that sell hardware are glad to help you buy the proper components. (Always ask about the return policy—30 days for substitutions and 15 days for returns are reasonable expectations.)

Okay, I made my list and paid a visit to a local computer store. I had a salesperson help me so I could be absolutely certain I was getting the right components. Note that a keyboard, mouse, and monitor/LCD are not included in the overall price. A mouse/keyboard combo can be purchased for about $10.00, and a monitor/LCD is a personal choice you'll need to make based on the size you want and the price you're comfortable with. In my case, I had a spare mouse/keyboard and an extra LCD panel from a much older retired PC.

■Note Space prevents me from providing details on each and every hardware purchase I made or why one component was selected over another. Computer building does require knowledge of how components work together, and I'll do my best throughout the chapter to explain my choices for purchasing a specific component. But if you're interested in learning more about how computers work and all the nitty-gritty details on computer hardware, I recommend a visit to http://www.webfreebees.net/ howtobuildpc.html. You can find discussions there on all the components used in the U-PC—plus many more.

I purchased the following for a total of $203.00 (see Figure 1-1):

- 1 black case with built-in 300-watt power supply: $39.00

- 1 ATX motherboard (built-in video, sound, network card and AM2 socket): $44.00

- 1 AMD 1300 processor 2.3GHz for an AM2 socket: $44.00

- 1 Western digital hard drive, 160GM capacity: $39.00

- 1 Crucial RAM memory chip, 1GB capacity: $13.00

- 1 CD/DVD-RW: $24.00

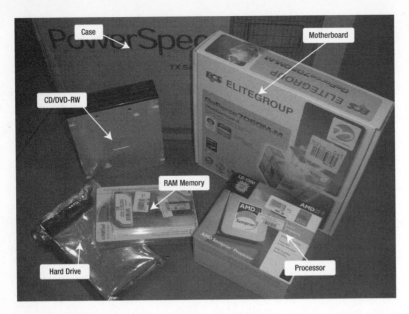

Figure 1-1. *My U-PC components came in a variety of bags, plastic containers, and boxes.*

Also included with the case are the power cord (to plug into the wall) and all the cables that will connect to the components: the hard drive, CD/DVD drive, processor, and so on.

My overall goal, of course, was to keep my costs low while meeting the minimum hardware requirements needed by Ubuntu (and listed earlier in the chapter). In many instances, it was impossible to purchase components near the recommended requirements; for example, Ubuntu requires 8GB of hard drive space, but the smallest capacity hard drive I could find was 80GB. The 160GB hard drive I ended up purchasing was only $5.00 more than the 80GB drive, so I ended up spending a few extra dollars for double the storage space. This was also the case with RAM—memory chips were not sold in anything less than 512MB, even though Ubuntu requires only 384MB.

■**Note** When purchasing a case, always make certain that it comes with a power supply. If it doesn't, you have to purchase one. Don't skimp here—go for a minimum of 300 watts or higher. The power supply comes with all the power cables that connect to your hardware components.

I might have all the parts of my U-PC, but until I put them together, they won't be of much use.

Putting It All Together

If you're going to follow along with my instructions and build your own U-PC, you might be a little nervous or concerned, especially if you've never built a computer before. So let me reveal a dirty little secret that most computer salespeople don't want you to know:

With a Phillips head screwdriver and a little patience, building your own PC is a piece of cake.

I'm not kidding. Follow along with my steps, and when your U-PC assembly is done, I'm betting you'll be asking "Is that all there is to it?" (Okay, so maybe you won't be asking that, but I promise that it doesn't get more complicated than the following steps, and I'm not a computer building expert. If I can do it, so can you.)

And here we go . . .

U-PC ASSEMBLY STEPS IN A NUTSHELL

1. Open all the components and sort them out, including any screws, cables, and so on.

2. Install the processor (and the processor's cooling fan) on the MB.

3. Install the RAM memory on the MB.

4. Open the computer case.

5. Install the MB.

6. Install the CD/DVD drive.

7. Install the hard drive.

8. Connect all cables from the power supply to individual hardware components.

9. Connect a keyboard, mouse, and monitor/LCD, and turn on the computer for a test.

10. Close up the computer case.

Step 1: Taking an Inventory of the Components

This was actually a fun step—it felt like it was my birthday when I opened all the boxes and bags and pulled out the shiny new parts. Figure 1-2 shows all the major parts of my U-PC. They're not so scary. (I left the MB and the processor in their protective containers; static electricity is a serious threat to some computer components and keeping them in their bags protect them from static charge until needed. That little pop you sometimes get when touching a doorknob is enough to damage a MB or RAM chip, believe it or not.)

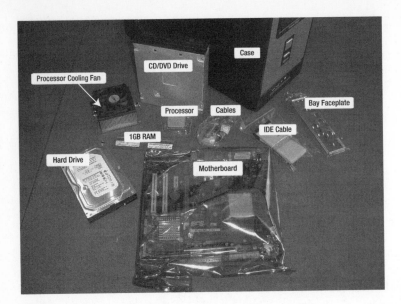

Figure 1-2. *All my U-PC components are opened and ready for assembly.*

■Caution When dealing with computer parts, always be aware that small amounts of static electricity have built up on your body. Even this small electrical charge is enough to damage some of these computer components. To prevent this type of damage, I recommend that you always touch something to discharge this static electricity (options include the metal external cover on the computer case or even a chair or table leg). Do this occasionally as you build your computer. Don't touch a monitor/LCD panel, however, because screens are notorious for static buildup instead of removing a static charge.

Step 2: Installing the Processor and Cooling Fan

I opened the MB and set it carefully down on the foam that came in the bag. I also touched my computer case to discharge any static electricity that might have built up. (The processor can be installed on the MB only one way, so be sure to read the documentation that comes with your processor and/or MB to determine the proper orientation and method for inserting your processor.)

■Tip When purchasing a processor, you'll probably end up purchasing either an Intel or AMD product. Cost is one factor; another is compatibility. All MBs come with a place to insert the processor. Because processors come in different shapes and sizes, it's important that you purchase a processor that matches the MB's processor slot. My MB provides an AM2 socket, so I purchased an AMD processor that fits in that AM2 socket. Make certain that your processor and MB sockets match. For more information on socket sizes and types, visit `http://en.wikipedia.org/wiki/CPU_socket`.

For my AMD processor, a small gold triangle in one corner (see Figure 1-3) matched up with a small triangle printed on the MB. My instructions told me to lift up the lever on the processor's AM2 socket (also seen in Figure 1-3), place the processor in the socket, and then press down and lock the lever. Figure 1-4 shows the processor inserted and the lever locked.

Figure 1-3. *Lift the lever and insert the processor into the socket.*

Figure 1-4. *After inserting the processor, lock down the lever.*

Next, I needed to install the processor's cooling fan. Processors get extremely hot, so most processors are sold with cooling fans included. If your processor does not come with a cooling fan, be sure to purchase one; without it, your processor will most assuredly be damaged by heat and become useless. (This can happen in minutes, days, or hours, but it will happen, so be warned.)

■**Note**   When installing a cooling fan on top of a processor, documentation will frequently tell you to place a small amount of thermal paste on top of the processor before placing the cooling fan on top. Thermal paste can be purchased inexpensively from most computer stores. My cooling fan came with thermal paste already applied to the surface of the fan that touches the processor; check with a salesperson to see if yours does as well.

I followed the instructions that came with my processor and clamped the cooling fan down on top of the processor, as shown in Figure 1-5. A small locking arm (not visible in the figure) ensures that the fan is clamped down securely.

Figure 1-5. *Install the processor's cooling fan as described in the processor's documentation.*

Finally, I needed to connect the cooling fan's power cable to the MB. Figure 1-6 shows the cable connected (consult your MB's documentation for the location of this plug). The cooling fan's plug is written on my MB and is easy to locate: it says CPU FAN (visible in Figure 1-5).

Figure 1-6. *The cooling fan gets its power from the motherboard.*

Step 3: Installing RAM Memory

Installing RAM memory is super easy. Figure 1-7 shows one of the memory slots with the clamps opened. (My slots are labeled DIMM1 and DIMM2.) I inserted the chip(s) in the lowest slot first (DIMM1 in this instance). You can see DIMM2 labeled in Figure 1-9, but DIMM1 is obscured in Figure 1-8.

Figure 1-7. *Open the clamps on a memory slot before inserting a chip.*

Memory chips typically have a notch along the bottom edge (see Figure 1-8). This notch helps determine the proper way to insert the RAM memory chip (it fits in the slot only one way).

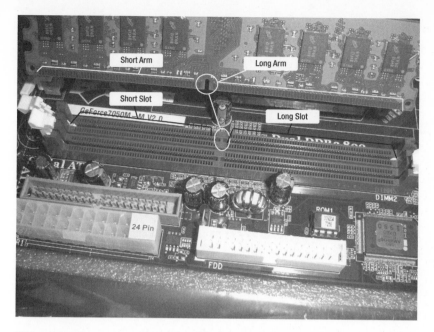

Figure 1-8. *The memory chip fits only one way in the slot.*

Figure 1-9 shows the RAM memory inserted. I pressed down firmly (but carefully) on the chip; the clamps closed and locked in the chip automatically.

Figure 1-9. *The clamps close and lock in the 1MB RAM memory chip.*

Step 4: Opening the Computer Case

My case has two sides that can be removed. How did I know which side to remove? Although I could remove both, I opened the side that allowed me to install the MB. (Once the MB is installed, the other side can be removed.) To find the right side, I looked on the rear of the case and opened the side farthest away from the slot and/or open bay shown in Figure 1-10. I simply removed the screws holding it and slid the side panel off. (Your case might use clips or some other method in place of screws; most cases are not complicated, so just look carefully and you should be able to determine how to remove the side.)

■Tip Earlier I mentioned that MBs and processors should be matched when it comes to the socket used by the processor. Well, your MB should also be matched to your computer case; it is called a *form factor*. Fortunately, today's cases are fairly typical in size (called an *ATX form*) and most MBs are, too. But just to be certain, make sure to verify that the form of your MB will fit inside your case. Visit http://en.wikipedia.org/wiki/Motherboard_form_factor for more information.

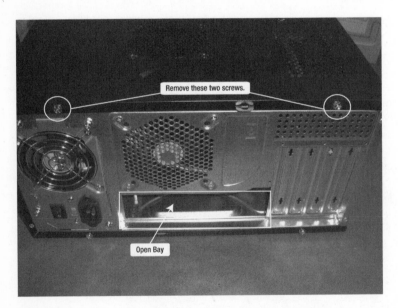

Figure 1-10. *Locate the screws and remove one side of the computer case.*

After removing the lid, I took a look inside. The inside of the case should look somewhat similar to the one shown in Figure 1-11. (My computer's power cord to plug into the wall was stored inside the case, but isn't shown in the figure.) If your case does not come with a power supply already installed, follow your power supply's instructions for connecting it to the case.

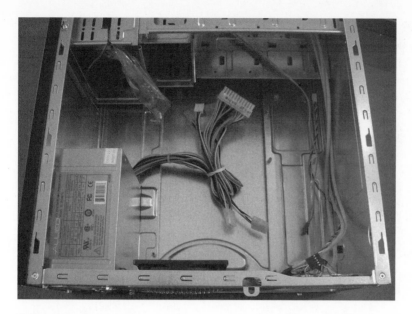

Figure 1-11. *The computer case is open and ready for parts to be added.*

If your MB comes with a small faceplate such as the one shown in Figure 1-12, insert it by pressing it against the bay opening (shown in Figure 1-10) from the inside. It should snap into place, as shown in Figure 1-13.

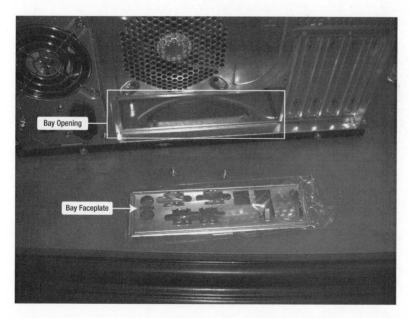

Figure 1-12. *Some motherboards come with a faceplate like this one.*

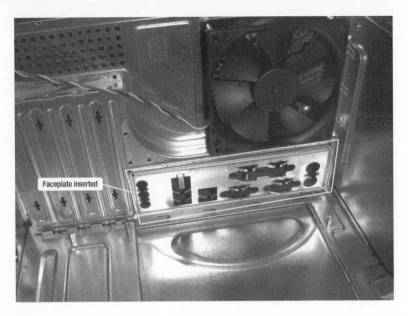

Figure 1-13. *The faceplate must be inserted in the case before connecting the motherboard.*

Step 5: Installing the Motherboard

Figure 1-14 shows the case with all the cabling moved out of the way. (Notice that there are a handful of mounting posts on the exposed side of the case.)

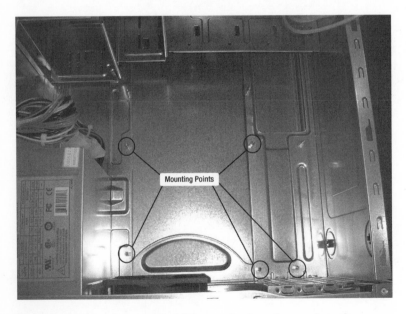

Figure 1-14. *Mounting posts hold the motherboard securely to the case.*

I carefully inserted the MB into the case (it's usually safe to grip it by the cooling fan and then lower it in), aligned the holes on the MB with the mounting posts, and used the screws that came with the case to secure the MB, as shown in Figure 1-15. (In some instances, not all mounting posts will be used, and some might not match up exactly; use as many as you can.)

Figure 1-15. *Screws and mounting posts hold the motherboard securely to the case.*

Step 6: Installing the CD/DVD Drive

I popped out one of the black panels on the front of the computer case (see Figure 1-16). I then reached inside the case and gently pushed against the panel—it popped out easily. This is where the CD/DVD drive will be inserted. (If you have multiple bay choices, pick the one you like best. I chose the top one because my case will be placed on the floor when in use.)

Figure 1-16. *Pop out one of the case's front bay panels for the CD/DVD drive.*

Next, I inserted the CD/DVD drive in the slot, as shown in Figure 1-17.

Figure 1-17. *Insert the CD/DVD drive into the open bay slot.*

I used the screws that came with the case to secure the CD/DVD drive to the case. To do this, I removed the other side of the case. With both sides open, I could insert the CD/DVD drive (and the hard drive in the next step) and secure them with screws on both sides, as shown in Figure 1-18.

■Note For both the CD/DVD and the hard drive, I highly recommend using as many screws as possible to secure them. Both drives contain spinning parts and over time the subtle vibrations they cause can loosen screws and/or cause a drive to move around. I used four screws per CD/DVD side (see Figure 1-18) and had no problems; likewise, I used two screws per side for the hard drive (see Figure 1-19).

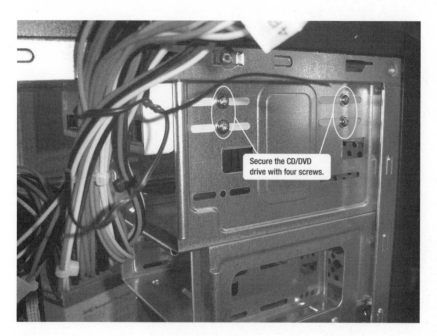

Figure 1-18. *Use screws to securely connect the CD/DVD to the case.*

Step 7: Installing the Hard Drive

The hard drive is inserted in the case from the inside. (You might have to experiment with locations for the hard drive because it will share a cable with the CD/DVD drive that connects to the MB.) For this reason, I chose to mount the hard drive in the highest drive spot in the case, as indicated in Figure 1-19. After I inserted the hard drive, I connected it to the case using only two screws per side, not three. If you have the option to connect using three screws per side, I highly recommend it.

■Tip Hard drives and CD/DVD drives connect to the MB using a special cable—typically either a SATA cable or an IDE cable (but others do exist). SATA drives and cables allow for faster data transfer, but cost more. Always check your MB specifications to determine whether it will support IDE or SATA (or both) and purchase a matching CD/DVD and hard drive. Your hard drive will typically come with the proper cable to connect it and the CD/DVD drive, but double-check this when you make the purchase. (Some MBs also include the proper cable.)

Figure 1-19. *Use screws to securely connect the hard drive to the case.*

Step 8: Connecting the Cables

There are *lots* of cables in the case, aren't there? This step can be the most frustrating, but with some patience and a checklist (provided as follows), it's not as difficult as it looks. The following must be connected and receiving power:

- The MB must be given power.

- The processor must be given power.

- The hard drive and the CD/DVD drive must be connected to the MB with special cable: either IDE or SATA (see previous Tip).

- The hard drive and CD/DVD drive must be given power.

- The power button and miscellaneous lights on the case front must be connected to the MB. (The miscellaneous lights are not required to be connected, but most motherboard documentation provides easy-to-follow instructions for this. Be patient; sometimes the connectors are small and can be tricky to connect.)

- Any USB ports on the case front must be connected to the MB.

- The case speaker must be connected to the MB.

- The case fan must be connected to the MB for power.

First, I connected power to the MB. The connector (shown in Figure 1-20) has a special shape that fits in only one place on the MB. Figure 1-21 shows the plug where the MB connector attaches. Again, don't force it; the connector is shaped so that it connects properly in only one way (this is the same for all other power connectors, too).

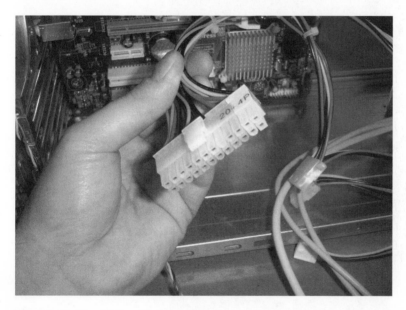

Figure 1-20. *The ATX motherboard power connector looks like this one.*

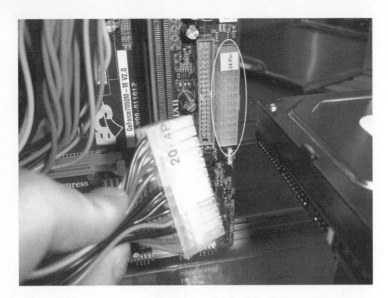

Figure 1-21. *The ATX motherboard power connector plugs in here.*

I found the secondary power connector coming from the power supply that fits the location shown in Figure 1-22. There's only one connector that has this shape, and the plug is located close to the processor.

Figure 1-22. *The secondary power connection*

I then located the special data cable shown in Figure 1-23. This data cable is used to connect the CD/DVD and the hard drive to the MB. There should be a red line along one edge (other colors are possible, too). When this cable is connected to the CD/DVD and the hard drive, the colored line must be facing the power connection on those drives (but again, the cable can really be connected only one way, so don't worry if your cable doesn't look exactly like this one).

Hard to see, but one edge will have a colored line running along it.

Figure 1-23. *The CD/DVD and the hard drive use this IDE cable to connect to the motherboard.*

One end of my data cable was blue; I located the blue plug on the MB and made the connection (see Figure 1-24).

Figure 1-24. *Connect the CD/DVD and hard drive cable to the motherboard.*

Next, I connected the hard drive to the data cable using the connector in the middle of the cable. I connected the remaining connector (on the end of the cable) to the CD/DVD drive. (You might have to move the CD/DVD drive and/or the hard drive to get them close enough for the cable connectors to properly connect; another option is to purchase a longer data cable from a computer store.) Figure 1-25 shows my data cable connected to both drives.

Figure 1-25. *The data cable is connected to the CD/DVD drive and hard drive.*

The CD/DVD drive and hard drive must now be given power. I located the power connectors, called *Molex connectors* (see Figure 1-26).

Figure 1-26. *Molex connectors provide power to the CD/DVD drive and hard drive.*

I found two Molex power cables and connected them to the CD/DVD drive and the hard drive, as shown in Figure 1-27.

Figure 1-27. *The Molex cables are connected to the CD/DVD drive and hard drive.*

The case has a small cable like the one shown in Figure 1-28. This cable connects the power button and lights on the front of the case to the MB.

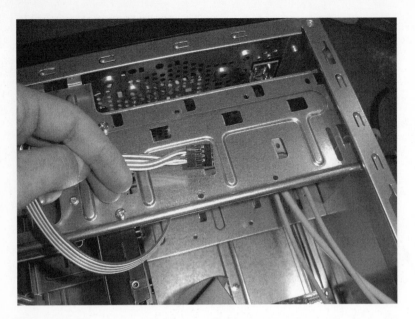

Figure 1-28. *The case's power button and lights are controlled by this cable.*

There's a plug located on my MB labeled PANEL1 where this connection was made. Consult your MB's documentation if you have any difficulty locating where this cable will connect. Figure 1-29 shows the cable plugged in.

Figure 1-29. *Plug in the case's power button and light controlling cable.*

If your case has one or more USB ports on the front (my case does), you have to locate the cable(s) coming from the front of the case and plug them into the MB. Look carefully at Figure 1-29; you should see some connections labeled USB1 and USB3; the USB cable(s) connect to them. Figure 1-30 shows my USB cable plugged into USB3. (If you have only one cable, it can plug into any of the USB connections with no problem.)

Figure 1-30. *Plug in the USB cable to one of the USB connectors.*

The last two things to connect were the case's speaker cable (coming out of the front of the case) and the case's rear fan. Figure 1-31 shows where these two final connections were made. On my MB, they are labeled SYS FAN and AUDIO. (Consult your MB's documentation for these locations if you're having trouble finding them.)

Figure 1-31. *The case's fan and speaker need to be connected to the motherboard.*

Figure 1-32 shows the case's speaker cable connected, and Figure 1-33 shows the case's fan cable connected.

Figure 1-32. *Connect the speaker cable to the motherboard.*

Figure 1-33. *Connect the case's fan to the motherboard.*

Step 9: Testing the U-PC

I connected a keyboard, mouse, and monitor; plugged in the computer; and then turned it on. Because there was no operating system installed, I saw a warning message (see Figure 1-34). This message simply says that the computer doesn't know where to find its operating system, or at least a bootable CD/DVD. (This process will be handled in Chapter 2.)

FATAL: No bootable medium found! System halted.

Figure 1-34. *The U-PC tells you it needs an operating system installed.*

TROUBLE WITH YOUR U-PC?

If you followed the steps along with me, did you get some other errors? First, look inside and make certain that both fans are spinning—the one on the processor and the one built into the power supply. You might not be getting power. Is there a light on the front of the case? Usually one of the lights blinks on and off to indicate the hard drive is working, but many errors cause the light to stay solid. Go back and check all your connections: make sure that all power cables are pushed in correctly (and tightly) and that the data cable is properly connected to the hard drive and CD/DVD drive. Make certain that the motherboard and processor are both receiving power from the power supply (refer to step 8) and that you used the proper power connectors in the proper locations.

Other methods for verifying a working U-PC include ensuring that the LED light on the ATX motherboard is lit (indicating that power is being received by the MB), checking that the BIOS setup is accessible (check your MB's documentation), and finally booting up a working Ubuntu operating system from the CD (see Chapter 2 for more details).

Is the computer still not working? Don't panic. Computers are fairly rugged these days, and the most likely problem is a loose or improper connection, or a cable that has been plugged into the wrong location. Start by returning to step 8 and double-checking all your connections—you might even consider unplugging everything and starting over. Your power supply most likely has unused power cables; feel free to use a different power connector—maybe the one you were using doesn't fit properly or is just "bad." The thing to remember is that you have a minimum number of components to check and it's likely that you'll find the culprit during a second visit.

If after you double- and triple-check the connections your computer is still not working, you have a few options. If you purchased your computer parts locally, you might call the store and ask if you can bring it in for someone to quickly look over. My local computer store has some really helpful employees who enjoy helping customers solve problems. If you bought the parts online, however, you might have to resort to having your computer looked at by a professional. (I know that's not the answer you want to hear, but consider how much money you're saving by buying the parts and building the computer yourself. Hiring someone at a reasonable hourly rate to look over your work can help find the problem and you'll most likely learn something, too. And the total cost of your U-PC plus a technician's fee will still be less than what you'd spend on a new computer from a store, right?)

Another resource is a local Linux user group. These groups usually consist of Linux hobbyists and professionals, and members are usually very patient and helpful with new Ubuntu Linux users trying to get a computer working and ready for an Ubuntu installation.

Step 10: Closing the Computer Case

This step is easy; I just put the case sides back on and screwed them down securely. (You can reconnect them using whatever method your case uses for keeping the sides from falling off.)

All that's left is to move the U-PC to its final location. Well, almost . . . it's time to begin the next part of the process: installing an operating system.

What's Next?

Congratulations! If you've gathered the parts and assembled them as I've described, you've got a great little computer that's ready for a great operating system: Ubuntu. In Chapter 2, I'll provide you with detailed steps for installing Ubuntu on your new computer. After the operating system is installed, the sky's the limit, as they say. So much software (free software!) is waiting for you to download, install, and use: business software, productivity software, game software, and more.

But I'm getting ahead of myself; first you'll get Ubuntu installed on your new U-PC and learn a little more about how it works. (And if you're a Windows user, you'll be pleasantly surprised at how easy the transition is to Ubuntu.)

CHAPTER 2

■■■

The Ubuntu Operating System

Whether you have decided to build your own U-PC, as I described in Chapter 1, or elected to use an existing computer, this chapter will provide you with the basic information you need to obtain the Ubuntu operating system and install it on the PC of your choice.

In the pages that follow, I'll provide a detailed walkthrough of the screens you will encounter during the installation and the desktop you will see after the operating system is up and running. But before all this can happen, you have to obtain a copy of the Ubuntu operating system (OS). There are three ways to do this, and they are covered in detail in Appendix B at the end of this book.

After you obtain your CD or DVD containing the Ubuntu installation files, grab a chair near your computer and let me show you how amazingly easy it is to get Ubuntu installed and working.

An Installation Overview

There's nothing complicated about installing Ubuntu. In fact, if you've ever performed an installation of the Microsoft Windows operating system, you'll be shocked at how simple and fast the Ubuntu install is when compared with its Windows counterpart.

■**Note** An Ubuntu installation doesn't always go smoothly, but the U-PC hardware I purchased (covered in Chapter 1) is fully compatible with Ubuntu, and the installation I performed and will cover shortly went off without a hitch. I'll show you in a bit how to test Ubuntu on your own computer without installing any files on your hard drive, which lets you take the OS for a test drive and ensures that certain things are working before you move forward. And, just in case there are problems, I'll provide some troubleshooting tips at the end of the chapter as well as some web sites you can visit for help.

Following is a short summary of what will happen in this chapter. Each of the following steps in this summary will then be covered in more detail later in the chapter:

1. Inserting the Ubuntu CD/DVD in the CD/DVD drive and turning on the computer

2. Selecting the language

3. Trying Ubuntu first without making any changes to the computer

4. Testing various items: sound, video, and network connectivity

5. Configuring the hard drive partition

6. Installing Ubuntu files on the hard drive

7. Logging in

8. Taking a tour of Ubuntu

■**Note** You might need to configure the motherboard's bootup settings to check for a CD/DVD inserted in the CD/DVD drive. Consult the motherboard documentation for instructions on setting the *boot device order*. This setting simply defines the order in which the computer will look for operating system files to load; typically you want your operating system to be started from a hard drive, but with a new computer there is usually no data on the hard drive. So you must tell your computer to look for OS files on a CD/DVD. Your Ubuntu CD/DVD will contain the proper files for it to start up. (This is covered in more detail in the next section.)

Ubuntu Installation

If your U-PC is built and ready to go, it's time to get Ubuntu installed. For purposes of this chapter, I'll use the term *U-PC* in the steps, but don't let that confuse you—if you're using an existing computer, just perform the same steps.

Step 1. Inserting the Ubuntu CD/DVD and Turning on the Computer

The Ubuntu CD/DVD is also called an *Ubuntu Live disc*, so it can run the Ubuntu operating system from the disc itself and doesn't require installing any files on your hard drive. This is a perfect way to test the operating system's user interface and see how you like it. But it also offers you the ability to test the U-PC's hardware to see whether there are any compatibility issues.

Begin by turning on the U-PC. You haven't inserted the Ubuntu CD/DVD yet, so once the computer has booted up, you'll see the message shown in Figure 2-1.

FATAL: No bootable medium found! System halted.

Figure 2-1. *The U-PC lets you know that it doesn't have an operating system installed.*

Why Ubuntu uses the word *FATAL* is a mystery; in fact, the U-PC is just fine. It's the rest of the message that tells you what you need to know: *No bootable medium found!* (Your error message might differ—various motherboards have different warning messages when bootable files aren't found.)

To fix this, you simply have to provide the U-PC with some bootable files (the Ubuntu CD/DVD will provide them). Open the CD/DVD drive tray, place the Ubuntu disc on the tray, and close it. Next, turn off the U-PC and then turn it back on. (I configured my U-PC motherboard to look at the CD/DVD drive for a bootable disc before examining the hard drive for bootable files.) Lo and behold, the CD/DVD drive will begin to spin, and the little light on the front will flicker. Something's happening.

Step 2. Selecting the Language

Next, you're presented with a selection screen similar to the one shown in Figure 2-3. It's a listing of all the languages supported by Ubuntu. Use the up and down arrow keys to choose the language and then press the Enter key. (At this point during the installation, the mouse won't work; use the up and down arrow keys to make selections.)

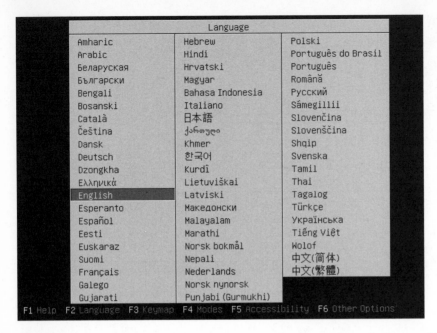

Figure 2-2. *Select the language you want to have Ubuntu use from the list provided.*

Step 3. Trying Ubuntu First Without Making Changes to the Computer

After the language is selected, Ubuntu displays a simple screen (see Figure 2-3). For now, ignore everything but the first option in the list labeled Try Ubuntu without any change to your computer. (It should be selected by default and displayed in white letters; all other options will be displayed in an orange-brown color. Use the up and down arrows to select this option if it's not already selected.)

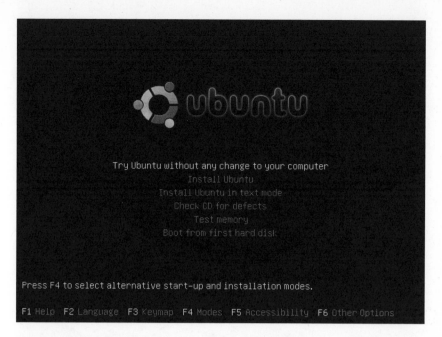

Figure 2-3. *Selecting the first option lets you test Ubuntu without risk to your computer.*

After making the selection, the CD/DVD drive begins to read files on the disc; Ubuntu is preparing to launch its desktop. This could take a few minutes or more; because files are not stored on your hard drive, all the information that the U-PC needs to run Ubuntu must be obtained from the disc and stored in RAM memory.

If there are any problems with Ubuntu running on your computer, you might see an occasional message on the screen. For now, just let the computer try and complete the Ubuntu desktop launch. If all goes as planned, the desktop opens, as shown in Figure 2-4 (and you should be able to use your mouse and keyboard).

Figure 2-4. *A clean Ubuntu desktop should appear on your screen.*

■**Note** The U-PC booted up from the Ubuntu Live disc with no problems, and the desktop appeared with no error messages. If any errors are reported during the bootup, write them down; later in the chapter I'll give you some options for different bootup configurations you can try, and these error messages might help you find a solution.

Step 4. Testing Various Items: Sound, Video, Network Connectivity

Once the Ubuntu desktop is up and running, it's time to try out a few things. Don't be afraid to click around and experiment; it's very difficult to do anything wrong when running Ubuntu from the CD/DVD—just don't click the Install icon on the desktop yet. Later in the chapter, I'll go over all the various menus and icons you see on the desktop, but first you should explore.

Before installing Ubuntu, you should perform three tests: video screen (the monitor or LCD), sound (the speakers), and Internet connectivity.

The video screen is easy: the desktop is in full color, and clicking the menus along the top of the screen opens and closes them. The motherboard provides a video signal to the LCD panel, so you'll be able to make sense of what you see on the screen.

Next, make sure that you can hear sounds and music from the speakers. To do this, double-click the Examples folder on the desktop (see Figure 2-4). Inside the Examples folder is a collection of sample files that test various applications. Find a file called `fables_01_01_aesop.spx`, as shown in Figure 2-5. Although the music bars are a huge hint that this is a sound file, the `.spx` file extension is used by the sound application that comes packaged with the Ubuntu installation (see Chapter 12 for more information).

Double-click the file and—sound! It's a narration of one of *Aesop's Fables* and it's crystal clear. So sound checks out.

■**Note** If you're not getting any sound, first make sure that your speakers are powered and plugged into the correct port on the back of your U-PC. Also check that the volume knob isn't set to zero or the lowest setting. If you're still not getting any sound, I provide some web sites and suggestions at the end of this chapter for troubleshooting problems and finding help.

Figure 2-5. *Find the Aesop's Fables sound file (with the .spx extension).*

The last test is to make certain you can access the Internet. If you have a broadband modem that lets you connect to the Internet, connect the network cable from the modem to the back of the U-PC. Now it's time to see if Ubuntu will let you browse the Internet.

To do this, click the small icon indicated in Figure 2-6. This icon launches Firefox, a free web browser that comes packaged with the Ubuntu installation files. I'll cover Firefox in more detail in Chapter 9, but for now all you want to do is make sure that you can get to the Internet.

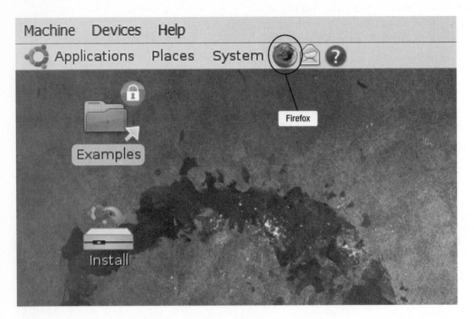

Figure 2-6. *Firefox verifies that the Internet connection is working.*

Firefox opens up; enter http://www.apress.com (this publisher's web site). After a few seconds, the web site appears (see Figure 2-7).

Figure 2-7. *Opening a web site lets you know that Ubuntu is working.*

This is great! Ubuntu appears to recognize the video, sound, and network hardware components. And you can use the mouse and keyboard, too. You know that the CD/DVD drive works because it loaded up Ubuntu. Now, all that's left is to prepare the hard drive to install the actual Ubuntu files on it. And to do that, you need to perform one more action from within Ubuntu: partitioning the hard drive.

Step 5. Partitioning the Hard Drive

You need to make certain that the hard drive is working properly. To do this, click the System menu, select the Administration option, and then click Partition Editor on the flyout menu, as shown in Figure 2-8.

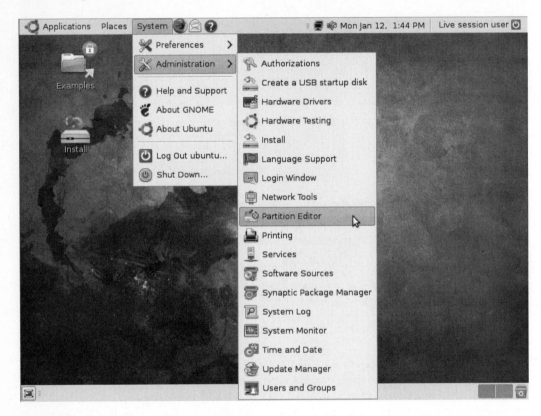

Figure 2-8. *Select Partition Editor from the System menu's Administration section.*

The Partition Editor opens, as shown in Figure 2-9.

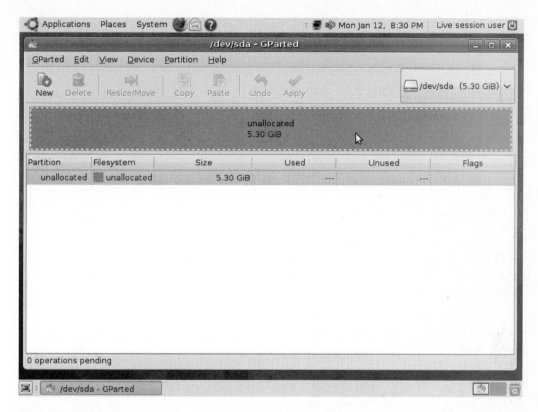

Figure 2-9. *Use the Partition Editor to prepare the hard drive for Ubuntu.*

My U-PC has a blank hard drive with 160GB of free space; yours might have more or less. Don't let this bother you; as long as you have a minimum of 8GB, you should be fine. Before that space can be used, however, a partition must be created in which the operating system will be installed.

Partitions can be a confusing topic, but fortunately Ubuntu and the Partition Editor handle most of the decisions for you. Think of your hard drive as a pie; uncut, the pie represents all the storage space on your hard drive lumped together in one big container with the Ubuntu operating system installed and all your files. It's one partition. But you can cut that pie up into sections, with each section set aside for a particular purpose—this is called *partitioning*. You can create a section for storing just your music files, for example, or even another section that can run an entirely different operating system! (This is called *dual booting*, and a PC like this will boot up and allow you to select which operating system you want to use.)

Tip Another consideration is the file system type. Windows and Linux don't use the same file system types. Windows usually uses NTFS, whereas the most common file system for Linux is ext3. Linux also needs a swap partition, which is really just a relatively small part of the hard drive acting as extra memory. Ubuntu community documentation has a nice explanation of file system types here: `https://help.ubuntu.com/community/LinuxFilesystemsExplained`. It also has a swap partition FAQ here: `https://help.ubuntu.com/community/SwapFaq`. When in doubt, let the Partition Editor handle things for you!

By default, the Partition Editor offers up the entire hard drive as one big container with no other sections. This is fine, and this is the method I'm using for my U-PC. But if you want to split your hard drive into say two sections of 80GB each (for a total of 160GB), you'll need to read through the Help documentation provided with Partition Editor. Click the Help menu and review the instructions for creating a new partition.

Note Why does Figure 2-9 show 5.30GiB (gigabytes) of space, not 160 gigabytes? To take screenshots of the Ubuntu install, I used special software called a *virtual machine (VM)* that allows me to perform an Ubuntu install on an existing computer's hard drive. I set aside 5.3GB of space (more than enough) on the computer's hard drive, and the VM software treats it as an unallocated hard drive for me to install the Ubuntu files. In reality, I performed the same steps on my real U-PC, but the Partition Editor shows 160GB of unallocated space, which is exactly what I expected.

To create a partition, click the line describing the partition to highlight it (indicated by the mouse arrow; refer to Figure 2-9) and then click the Partition menu and select New, as shown in Figure 2-10.

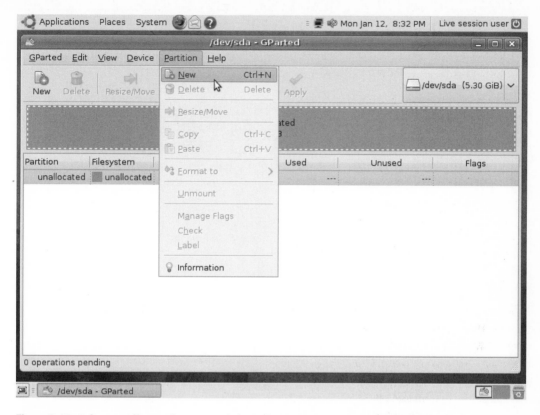

Figure 2-10. *Select unallocated space and then choose New to create a partition.*

A warning message appears, as shown in Figure 2-11. It is not a concern for this U-PC because the hard drive has no data on it, but if you're using an existing PC, be aware that any data you haven't backed up will be erased. Click the Create button to proceed.

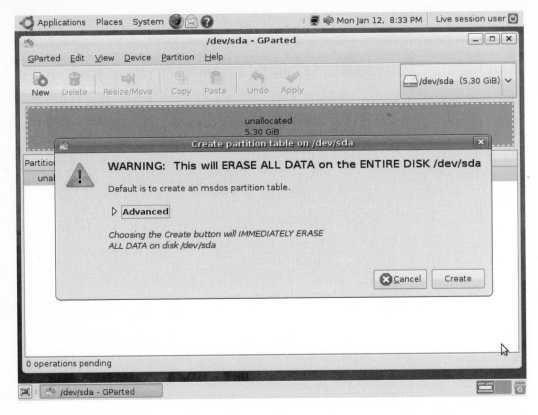

Figure 2-11. *A warning message lets you know that any data on the hard drive will be erased.*

Select the Partition menu again and click New. This time, a different window appears (see Figure 2-12).

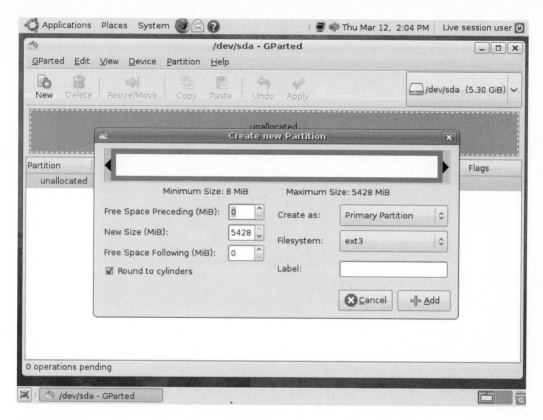

Figure 2-12. *Create the partition that will hold the Ubuntu operating system.*

Change the default Filesystem setting to **ext3** and click the Add button; this process creates a Primary Partition in which the operating system's files will reside (as well as any other files you create and save). The Partition Editor screen changes (see Figure 2-13), and the words New Partition #1 appear.

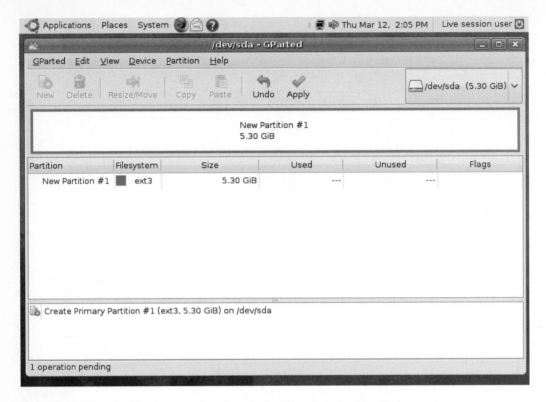

Figure 2-13. *The partition is created and ready for Ubuntu to be installed.*

Finally, click the Partition box (labeled New Partition #1 in Figure 2-13) and click the Apply button. You'll see a final warning message asking whether you're certain you want to continue (shown in Figure 2-14). Click the Apply button to finalize the creation of the partition.

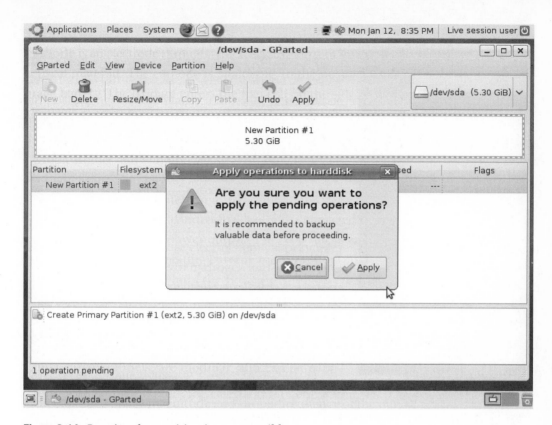

Figure 2-14. *Creating the partition is not reversible.*

Exit out of the Partition Editor by selecting the GParted menu and selecting Quit. This returns you to the Ubuntu desktop. Now you're ready to install Ubuntu on the hard drive.

Step 6. Installing Ubuntu Files on the Hard Drive

On the desktop is an icon labeled Install (refer to Figure 2-4). To install Ubuntu, you can simply double-click that icon, and the process begins.

A Welcome screen appears, as shown in Figure 2-15. Select the language (again) from the left side of the screen and click the Forward button to continue.

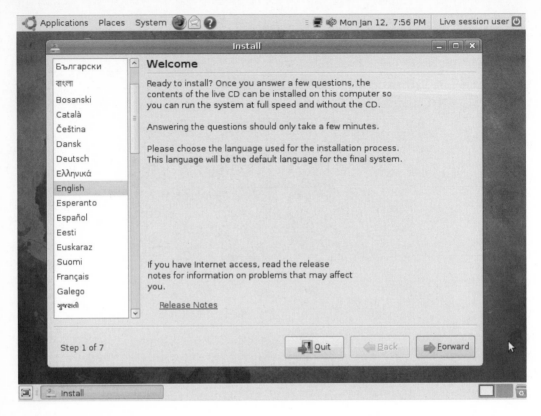

Figure 2-15. *Select the language as the first of seven steps to install Ubuntu.*

On the Where are you—screen shown in Figure 2-16, use the mouse to click the map and zoom in to your approximate location. The time zone will update based on your selection. Click the Forward button to continue.

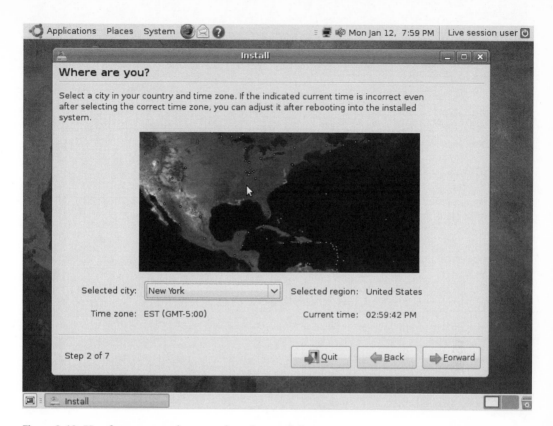

Figure 2-16. *Use the map to select your location and time zone.*

Now select the keyboard layout. Choose USA and click the Forward button to continue (see Figure 2-17).

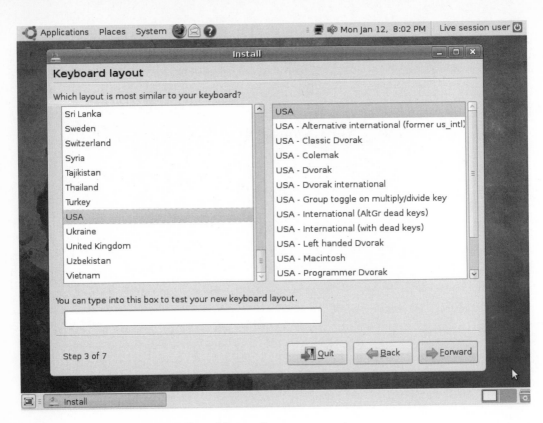

Figure 2-17. *Select the proper keyboard layout for your computer.*

Next, you're asked whether you want to do any additional partition work on the hard drive (see Figure 2-18). You already created the primary partition and don't need to make any changes, so click the Forward button to accept the default settings and continue. You'll see a warning that the changes cannot be undone. Click the Continue button; the hard drive spins a little, and the light blinks on and off for a few seconds—something good must be happening! (The hard drive spinning and the little light blinking tells you that files are being copied from the Ubuntu install disc to the hard drive, and things are proceeding as planned.)

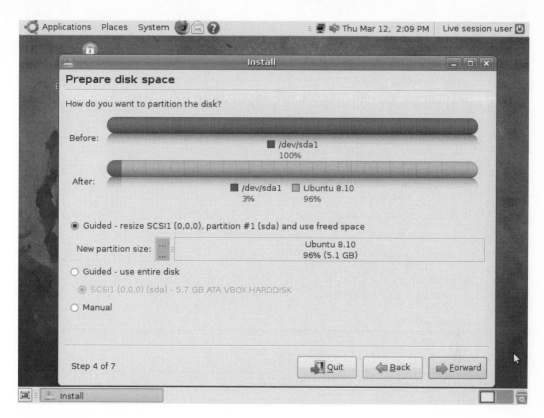

Figure 2-18. *Check that the partition is selected.*

On the Who are you? screen (see Figure 2-19), provide your name, a login name, a password (typed twice for verification), and the name of the computer.

For names I use **jim**, **jim**, and **jim-laptop**. Because I'll be sharing this computer with another user (my spouse), I leave the box labeled "Log in automatically" unchecked and click the Forward button.

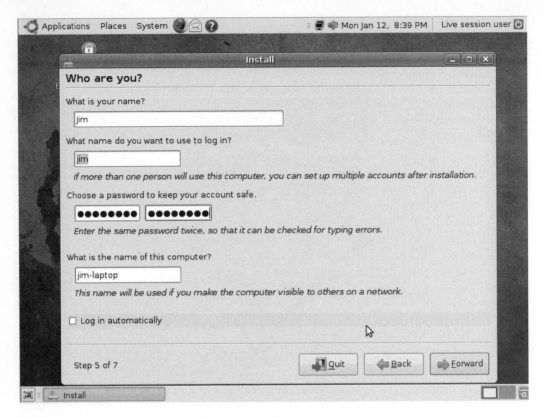

Figure 2-19. *Ubuntu needs some information to create a user account.*

Next, you see a summary of all the information provided or selected (see Figure 2-20). Click the Install button and let the installation proceed.

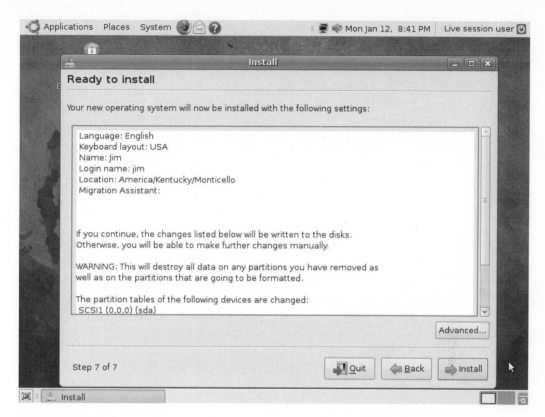

Figure 2-20. *Click the Install button to complete the installation of Ubuntu.*

■**Note** You might have noticed that the window shown in Figure 2-20 jumped from Step 5 of 7 (seen in Figure 2-19) to Step 7 of 7. You didn't do anything wrong and you didn't miss a step. Because only a Primary Partition was created back in Step 5, Step 6 was skipped. What is Step 6? If you choose to break your hard drive into multiple partitions, you will select in Step 6 on which partition to install the Ubuntu operating system boot files.

After you finish, the window shown in Figure 2-21 opens. (All in all, it took about 30 minutes for me to complete step 1 to step 6. The actual file copying took about 15 minutes on my U-PC.)

Figure 2-21. *Restart the computer to get Ubuntu up and running.*

Click the Restart now button and remove the Ubuntu disc from the CD/DVD drive. The computer will reboot and present you with a new login screen.

Step 7. Logging In

When Ubuntu first starts up, you see a username screen, as shown in Figure 2-22. Usernames are case sensitive, and after you type in your username (refer to Figure 2-19), you're asked to enter your password. If you provide the correct information, Ubuntu opens up to the familiar desktop and is ready to use.

Figure 2-22. *Provide a username and password to log in to Ubuntu.*

Step 8. Taking a Tour of Ubuntu

If you're at all familiar with Microsoft Windows or any other operating system with a graphical user interface, Ubuntu won't take long for you to learn to use. You click the left mouse button to select and drag items, you double-click the left mouse button to open files, and you right-click a file to see a flyout menu with additional options.

Let's take a quick look at some of the options available to you on the Ubuntu desktop, starting in the upper-left corner of the desktop (shown in Figure 2-23).

Figure 2-23. *A handful of menus and icons are available on the Ubuntu desktop*

In the upper-left corner are three menus and three small quick launch icons. From the left, the menus are Applications, Places, and System; followed by a small icon for the Firefox web browser (covered in Chapter 9), an e-mail icon to launch the Evolution e-mail application (see Chapter 4), and the Help icon to launch the built-in Ubuntu Help Center.

Click the Applications menu (shown in Figure 2-24) and you'll see seven preconfigured categories in which your applications can be organized, as well as an Add/Remove button that, well, lets you add and remove applications. Moving your mouse over a category launches a flyout menu that provides a list of possible applications for you to launch.

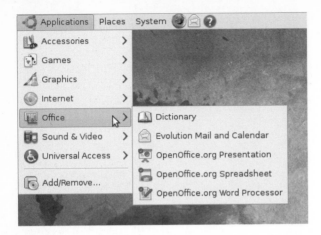

Figure 2-24. *Menus can contain categories with applications and other tools.*

The Places menu (shown in Figure 2-25) has many uses. Not only does it provide short-cuts to popular folders on your computer (such as the Music folder or the Documents folder), but it's also useful if you have multiple computers at your home or office with shared drives or folders. You can also access shared drives, folders, and files from this menu.

Figure 2-25. *The Places menu gives you quick access to folders and network locations.*

The System menu (see Figure 2-26) gives you access to the administrative tools needed to manage the Ubuntu computer. If you have ever used the Control Panel found in Microsoft

Windows, many of the items found in this menu should be familiar. The Preferences category has many options: you can change your wallpaper, set a screensaver, enable Bluetooth devices, and more.

The Administration category (also seen in Figure 2-26) controls more of the global options of Ubuntu that affect not only you but also any users on your computer. You can add new hardware, create new user accounts, change the system date and time, and more.

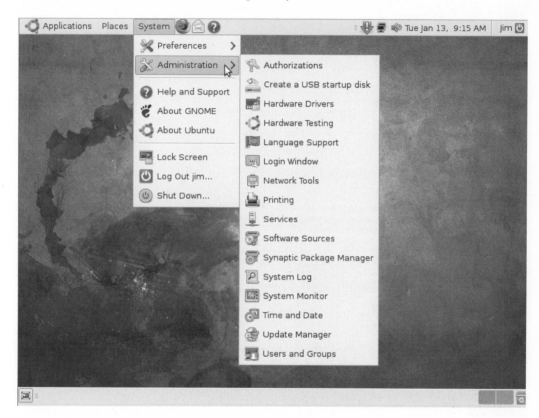

Figure 2-26. *The System menu contains dozens of administrative tools.*

Note There are entire books written just on the Ubuntu operating system and how to use it (see Appendix C). Also available are web sites that provide help to everyone from novice to guru (also found in Chapter 12 and at the end of this chapter). This book provides only a summary of how to navigate the Ubuntu operating system and to launch and use some of the included applications. If you have questions about any aspect of Ubuntu, the answers are out there, including more detailed coverage of each and every tool available in the System menu. Start by searching the Help Center (covered later in this chapter); you might be surprised by how much detail is provided there and on the official Ubuntu web site at http://www.ubuntu.com.

Returning to the Ubuntu quick launch icons to the right of the System menu, clicking either the Firefox or Evolution icon shown in Figure 2-23 will launch that application. Each of these applications is covered in its own chapter (Evolution in Chapter 4 and Firefox in Chapter 9), so please feel free to jump ahead if you want to begin using those applications now. Clicking the Help icon opens up the Ubuntu Help Center (see Figure 2-27).

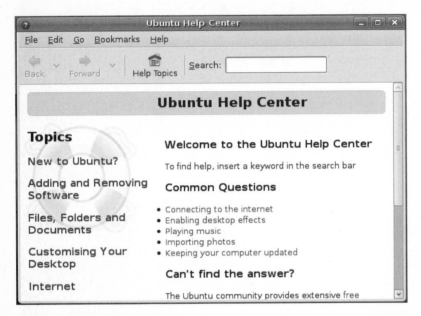

Figure 2-27. *The Ubuntu Help Center is a useful tool as you begin using Ubuntu.*

The Ubuntu Help Center is fully searchable using keywords: enter the keyword in the text box near the top and then press the Enter key. You'll be provided with a list of possible articles related to your query. You might also click individual topics along the left edge that can be used to view articles describing how to perform specific actions within Ubuntu. Finally, links are provided so you can submit your own questions or search for them on external web sites and forums if you can't find what you're looking for in the Ubuntu Help Center.

Now let's look at the upper-right corner of Ubuntu (see Figure 2-28).

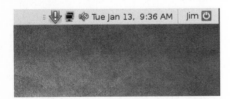

Figure 2-28. *Additional icons on the Ubuntu desktop provide information on running services.*

Starting from the left, you might or might not see the downward-pointing arrow with the exclamation mark on your desktop, but if you do, click it once. This icon will appear when there are updates to the Ubuntu system available. Many of these updates are security related and are released to protect your operating system from malicious sources such as viruses or attacks via an Internet connection. As you can see in Figure 2-29, after I clicked the Update icon, a new window opened, informing me that I have 219 updates that should be installed. This isn't out of the ordinary for a new installation of Ubuntu, and if you have a broadband connection, it won't take long for the updates to be installed.

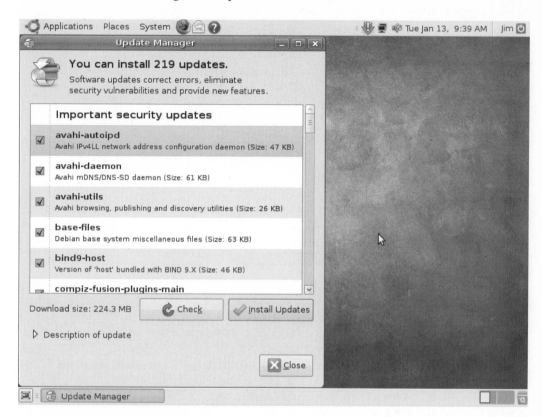

Figure 2-29. *I have a lot of updates that need to be installed on my operating system.*

The next icon from the left looks like two small computer screens overlapping. This Network icon gives you access to any of your network hardware, as well as the ability to configure it. If, for example, you install Ubuntu on a laptop that has both a wireless network card and a standard network card that uses a cable, you can use this icon to switch between the two by clicking it once and selecting the appropriate card.

To the right of the Network icon is the Sound icon; you can increase or decrease the volume of your speakers or mute the sound by clicking this icon once. Right-click the icon for additional options.

Finally, the date and time are provided. Click the date/time button to view the calendar or right-click the button to change the date or time, or perform other options.

The username of the person currently using Ubuntu is also available (refer to Figure 2-23). This is useful if multiple users will access a computer running Ubuntu; a quick glance can tell you if someone else has logged you out and logged in with a different user account.

The last item to cover on the Ubuntu desktop is seen in Figure 2-30. This is the status panel that is running along the bottom edge of the screen. It shows any current windows that are open (for example, Figure 2-30 shows that the Update Manager window is open, as shown in Figure 2-29). The button on the far left of the status panel, when clicked, will minimize (or hide) any open windows on the screen. It's a nice feature when you have a lot of clutter on your desktop; click the button and then find the window you want to use listed on the status panel. Click that window, and only that item will open on the desktop.

Figure 2-30. *The status panel runs along the bottom edge of the desktop.*

On the far right of the status panel are two small rectangles. One rectangle is shaded; it represents the desktop screen you are currently viewing. If you click the other rectangle, you can create a new "virtual" screen—it's like having a second monitor or LCD panel connected to your computer. (The only difference is that you must toggle back and forth between them instead of seeing them both at the same time.)

■**Tip** If you right-click either rectangle and choose the Preferences option, you can create up to 36 virtual screens!

The final icon on the far right of the status panel is the Trash icon. You can drag and drop files on this file and they'll be kept there until you empty it (by right-clicking and choosing Empty Trash). Click the icon once and it will open, allowing you to view any files that have been sent to the Trash.

And that's the desktop! Ubuntu is extremely easy to use—most menu selections are fairly self-explanatory (and there's always the Help Center if you can't figure out how to use an option). But Ubuntu by itself really isn't all that useful. Applications are where you'll be doing most of your work, and that's the focus for the remaining chapters in the book. I'll be covering many of the applications that came preinstalled with the Ubuntu installation in later chapters, but for now, feel free to take some time and get to know the Ubuntu operating system. Click some menus, launch some tools, and become familiar with how the OS operates.

Troubleshooting

Ubuntu is a very stable operating system. Problems during installation are rare, and if you do encounter them, there are some useful options available to push past any roadblocks and continue forward with the installation.

First, take a look at Figure 2-31 and then I'll explain some of the options to you.

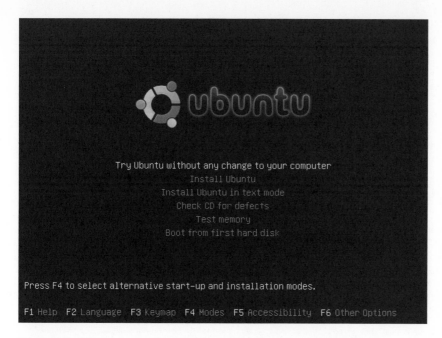

Figure 2-31. *Ubuntu provides tools for troubleshooting an installation.*

One of the first things you can do before beginning your installation is to select the fourth option in the list, labeled "Check CD for defects." Yes, sometimes a small scratch or defect on the surface of the disc can cause all sorts of problems. Selecting the "Test memory" option will make sure that your computer has the proper amount of RAM memory installed for Ubuntu to operate properly. These are simple quick tests you can perform before beginning the install.

What I call the troubleshooting power tools are found along the bottom edge of Figure 2-31. The F1 key (Help) does provide help, but it can be overly technical and (quite honestly) not as much "help" as you might need. The F4 key (Modes) is a frequent solution to many install problems because it deals with the video display. Display problems can cause many issues with an Ubuntu install, and an easy solution to push through is to select VGA as the video type. (Once you've got Ubuntu up and running, you can at least use the operating system while investigating why your video card isn't displaying at the proper resolution.) Again, display resolution is a common problem, so try this.

Finally, if you're having real difficulties getting Ubuntu to install, pressing F6 (Other Options) will give you access to some expert-level options. My recommendation is to post any error messages you might encounter during the install to one of the Ubuntu technical discussion forums (visit http://www.ubuntu.com/support/communitysupport); many of the Ubuntu experts who provide online help to new users will offer advice that involves the options found by pressing F6.

My final bit of advice is this: don't let Ubuntu frustrate you. Most of the time there's a solution for pushing past an install problem. Members of the Ubuntu user community are proud of this operating system, and they want it to grow and flourish and find new users. That said, the community has experts who are friendly and knowledgeable and willing to help you if you give them the chance. Be polite, be descriptive in typing up the problem, and be patient, and you should find a super-helpful collection of Ubuntu fans offering up advice to get you up and running.

What's Next?

Your Ubuntu installation comes with a nice collection of preinstalled software—all of it free. But what does "free" really mean? Are there hidden costs? Who pays for this software? And what else is available?

Before I begin covering specific software that works with Ubuntu, however, I'll take a short break in Chapter 3 and talk about types of free software, how to find it, where to get it, and some of the challenges in using it. Free software doesn't mean free of bugs, however, and you have to be able to distinguish the junk from the jewels. You're already off to a good start with a 100 percent free operating system, and my aim in Chapter 3 is to show that you might very well never have to pay for software to install on Ubuntu . . . ever.

CHAPTER 3

■ ■ ■

Free Software Defined

I hope you now have the Ubuntu operating system installed and are beginning to wonder about the possible uses it can provide. But if you're not yet convinced that a free operating system can compete with a big name operating system (BNOS), maybe this chapter (and the remaining chapters) will finally convince you to install Ubuntu.

Have you taken a look at the prices of software these days? Productivity applications (such as Microsoft Office) can easily exceed $300.00, and the most popular photo editing and graphic design applications are pushing $500.00 and higher! And what about the personal finance software that's supposed to help you monitor your bank account and get control of your spending? You'll be forking out $70.00 or more for those types of applications.

Or maybe not. Ever since someone slapped a price on a piece of software, someone else has offered a competing product for less—often for free. And it's that last part that this book is all about. In Chapter 1, I managed to build an ultra-low-cost computer (the U-PC); in Chapter 2, I showed you how to install a 100 percent free operating system on it.

Can you continue to keep the expenses down as you load up the U-PC with software?
Of course!
How?
Keep reading.

Application Types

I'm oversimplifying this a bit, but keep in mind that there are four types of software:

- Pay-to-use software (whether you pay a flat fee or a subscription)

- Open source software (with no hidden costs—nothing, zero, nada, zip)

- Cloud computing software (free, but possibly with a catch)

- Freeware (free, but with no guarantees of quality or virus-free installation)

I'll be providing a little more details in a bit to help you better distinguish between the four types. But for now, I need you to understand that when it comes to software, you have two options: you can pay for the software you use or you find free alternatives. Many people find a nice balance between the two, paying for software that they "can't live without" and loading up free software that they find on the Internet.

■Note I don't count pirated software that you might get from your third cousin's best friend's part-time auto mechanic as free. Don't steal software—there's simply no reason for it because tons of free applications exist that can probably do the job.

So, I'll now provide more details about those four software types and explain how to distinguish between them.

Pay-to-Use Software

This section won't be long, I promise. With *pay-to-use software*, you visit your local computer store or a big name chain store, find a box containing the software you want to install on your computer, and your bank account balance is then lowered anywhere from $20.00 to $600.00.

Another version of pay-to-use software is found when you visit a company's web site, provide your credit card information, and then download the software immediately using your broadband connection. (Sometimes you have to wait for the company to actually send you the software on a disc—anxiously checking your mailbox daily for its arrival.) With the downloadable software, you get no CD/DVD disc, no printed manual, and no pretty box with color graphics on the front. Would you believe, however, that you're probably charged the same amount of money as if you'd purchased the boxed version from a brick-and-mortar store? It's happened to me! You'll typically get no explanation for why you're not getting a discount for saving them packing and shipping costs.

Finally, there's another version of pay-to-use that's even more devious: *subscription software*. You pay a one-time product initiation fee (typically large) to get the software and then you pay a weekly/monthly/yearly *subscription fee* (sometimes also referred to as a *maintenance fee*) to keep using the software.

■Note Sometimes this fee can be a valid cost, such as for an antivirus application. The company provides regular updates to the software because of the 500 new viruses that are created each day. But most often, this is simply another money maker for the big software companies (see Figure 3-1).

Trend Micro? Internet Security Bulletin:
Online Peace Of Mind For Only $3.25 Per Month

Dear James,
Your Trend Micro PC-cillin? Internet Security expires in **02 Weeks!**

Click here to renew your protection now!

50% off
When You Renew
Before Expiration!

Renew Later:
~~$79.00~~

Renew Now:
$39.00

Renew Now

Protects up to 3 PCs
With free upgrade to
Trend Micro
PC-cillin? Internet Security 16

Expiring Product:
Trend Micro PC-cillin Internet Security 12

Expiring Serial Number:

Expiration Date:
Sunday, 18th January 2009

You don't leave your purse or wallet unattended on a public beach.
You take simple precautions to protect your property. We recommend that you treat your Dell with as much care as you would any other important possession. For $39.00 a year ($3.25 per month) you can enjoy the peace of mind that comes with knowing that your personal information, financial files, and private passwords continue to be protected by Trend Micro Software.

Take a few minutes to Renew and Upgrade for **$3.25 per month!**

Thank you,
Trend Micro

Figure 3-1. *Most antivirus applications charge a yearly subscription fee.*

Believe it or not, the current rumors buzzing around the technology world are that subscription software is the future of software: you won't buy software anymore; you'll "rent" it. Miss a payment and that software might very well uninstall itself from your computer, requiring a completely new purchase (with that large product initiation fee) before starting up with the subscription fees again.

Shocked? Angry? Confused? Yes to all three? Well, let me put your mind at ease and let you know that there are individuals, teams, and companies out there determined to fight subscription fees every step of the way. And they're doing this by creating free applications that are competing with the big name applications (BNAs).

Open Source Software

Open source software is the real deal: quality software that you can have at zero cost, with no advertisements or hidden subscription fees, no spyware that installs itself on your computer and monitors your activities, and no weekly e-mail asking you to upgrade to the latest version for a small fee.

Caution You can perform a Google search using the keywords "free software" and you'll get more than 200 million hits (try it). Sadly, most of the "free" software you'll find isn't free. There is shareware software that you can download and use for 30 days (free), but often it has some features disabled that come alive only when you purchase the full version. There is also trialware software that does give you the full version of an application (usually for 30 days or less), but locks up when the trial period ends. And the worst scam of all is the software labeled "free" that allows you to download and install the software (for free), but doesn't run until you submit credit card information. Add to all this subterfuge the fact that free software often has viruses and other malicious software hidden inside. The lesson here is that "free software" can often be misleading and sometimes even downright dangerous to the health of your computer. So beware!

How do you find the real deal? Well, the two words I want you to keep in mind as you move forward in the book are *open source*. I won't drown you with philosophical or theoretical discussions on the meaning of open source; if you're really interested, I highly recommend that you visit `http://www.opensource.org/` (see Figure 3-2) and spend some time learning about the concept, how it works, and why it's important to you.

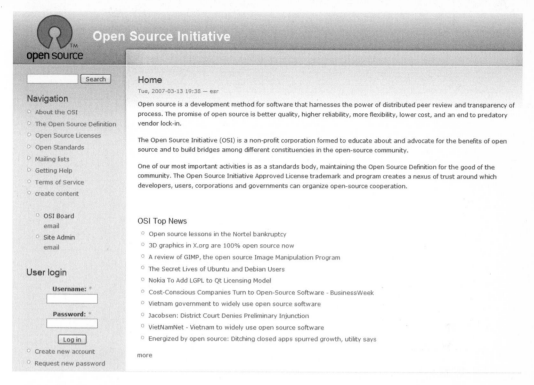

Figure 3-2. *Open Source Initiative is a great resource for learning about the open source movement.*

For now, however, the term *open source* should be something you always add to your Google search when looking for software: "open source games," "open source finance software," "open source recipe software"—get the picture?

Free software does exist that is not labeled open source, and you'll have to do some research on your own to determine whether there are any risks involved with downloading and installing it, not to mention determining whether it's actually free (see the next section for more information). But it's the open source stuff that's typically safe to download, safe to install, and safe to use. Why? Because open source software doesn't hide its inner programming (also called *code*) from the public. It's free to examine for errors and malicious code; the open source programmers allow this as a way to improve, troubleshoot, and verify their software. (Of course, you ideally need to be a programmer to verify the code—I'm not a programmer, but all I have to do is a quick Google search on the application and I can quickly determine whether there is anything shady going on with the application in question.)

Much of the software covered in this book (and that comes bundled with the Ubuntu installation) is open source: OpenOffice.org (similar to the Microsoft Office suite of applications, as seen in Figure 3-3), GIMP (a photo/graphics editor), and Evolution (an e-mail app) are all open source. But what about the software I cover that isn't open source? Well, that falls into the third category of software.

Figure 3-3. *OpenOffice.org offers a bundle of applications to compete with Microsoft Office.*

Cloud Computing Software* (always read the small print)

Don't you just hate asterisks and "the small print?" During the installation of most software, you're typically stopped at some point to acknowledge a user license agreement or some legal mumbo-jumbo: "Click the Yes button to accept the agreement or the No button to cancel the installation." (Even open source software has this agreement, but 99.9 percent of the time it's to make sure you acknowledge the fact that the software is to *remain free.*)

Believe it or not, a lot of free software exists that is high in quality and won't cost you a penny. *Cloud computing* is all the rage these days, and if you think you don't know what it is, you're probably wrong. Let me explain.

Do you use your Internet connection to check your bank balance (also called *Internet banking*)? (Even if you don't, you're probably familiar with the concept.) When you visit http://www.myownpersonalbank.com and enter your username and password, the screen displays your current balance, maybe the last dozen checks you've written, and perhaps a few of your debit card charges at the local coffee shop. Is that financial information you're viewing stored on your computer's hard drive? Probably not. Instead, that information is kept secured (hopefully) on a hard drive owned by your bank. That hard drive might be down the road, in a different state, or even possibly in a different country! But by providing a simple username and password, your web browser presents your personal financial information to you on the screen with possible options that include printing a statement, transferring funds from a checking account to savings, and even viewing scanned images of your checks (see Figure 3-4).

Transaction History

◀ Return to Your Accounts

About FREE BUSINESS CHECKING - 0947

Statements

Download transactions...

Order checks...

Order check copy...

Request stop payment

Make a loan payment

Alerts & Notification Settings

About this account

🖨 Print this page

Have Questions?

Does Washington Mutual offer guideline checks and account statements in accessible formats for customers with visual impairments?

How can I view an image of my check online?

What kind of problem could cause my check image to be "unavailable"?

Ask your question here...

TIP Now you have ac

Free Business Checking - 0947   Select an acc

▶ **Available Balance** : $▇▇▇

Search by: Date Range ▼ ➡ From: ▢

Search for last: 30 days | 60 da

Date ▼	Description	Check#
1/16/2009	OPPENHEIMER CPS PURCHS ▇▇▇	
1/14/2009	*CUSTOMER DEPOSIT	
1/13/2009	Check - 0000001202	1202📷
1/12/2009	AMERICAN EXPRESS ELEC REMIT ▇▇▇	
1/8/2009	Check - 0000001201	1201📷
12/23/2008	Check - 0000001120	1120📷
12/16/2008	OPPENHEIMER CPS PURCHS ▇▇▇	
12/16/2008	*CUSTOMER DEPOSIT	
12/10/2008	AMERICAN EXPRESS ELEC REMIT ▇▇▇	
12/9/2008	Check - 0000001119	1119📷
11/24/2008	*CUSTOMER DEPOSIT	
11/18/2008	OPPENHEIMER CPS PURCHS ▇▇▇	
11/10/2008	AMERICAN EXPRESS ELEC REMIT ▇▇▇	
11/3/2008	Check - 0000001116	1116📷

Figure 3-4. *Clicking the camera icons lets me view my checks.*

This is an example of cloud computing, where the cloud is the Internet. You use your computer's web browser and Internet connectivity to use software applications that exist on computers located "somewhere else." Besides Internet banking, cloud computing examples include web-based e-mail (such as Google Mail, Hotmail, and Yahoo! Mail), video streaming (YouTube is the big name here: http://www.youtube.com), and even online gaming such as playing poker with human players from around the world. These services don't require you to install software on your computer; you simply enter the web address (URL), the web site loads the required application in your web browser, and away you go.

■**Caution** Cloud computing does have one very large risk. Because you're often accessing personal information that's for your eyes only (banking, e-mail, and so on), your connection to the service provider is only as good as the password you're using. If your username is your first name, and your password is your spouse's birthday (the *mm/yy* format is popular, such as *0401* for April 1), how easy do you think it might be for a bad guy to gain access to your information? (You should also be aware that teenagers are master password crackers, so maybe **#1Dad** isn't the best password, huh?)

But if so many of the cloud computing applications don't cost any money, you might already be wondering how businesses that offer these services can do so for free. And that's where the asterisk comes in.

Most cloud computing services that are free to you (the customer) are paid for by advertisers. Sometimes these advertisements are small and unobtrusive, maybe hidden in the lower-right corner of the screen where you will never notice them. Other times, the advertisements exist as banner ads that run across the top of the page (and sometimes down both sides and in the middle, as shown in Figure 3-5.)

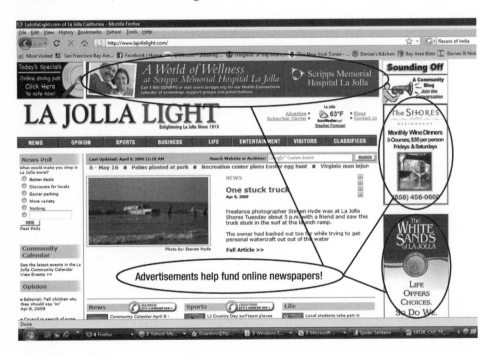

Figure 3-5. *Find all the advertisements and you win a prize.*

One of the biggest cloud computing service providers is one you already know: Google. Google offers so many free services via web browsers that I've stopped counting. It has a word processor app, a spreadsheet app, a web design app, an e-mail app . . . and the list goes on. (See Chapters 10 and 11 for more information on some of Google's free apps.)

I mentioned earlier in the chapter that rumors are all pointing to software moving to a subscription format. Well, the rumors are also pointing to more and more cloud computing applications appearing. This means you'll soon be seeing pay-to-use-cloud-computing as companies begin to figure out how to charge you money for what is typically available today for free but is advertiser-sponsored.

Freeware (or Everything Else)

The last bit of free software that I want to cover doesn't really fall under the open source or cloud computing umbrella. This software, which is typically labeled *freeware*, can be found all over the Internet by doing a Google search for "freeware." But beware—you'll get millions of search returns for that label, and most of them aren't worth a click of your mouse to investigate.

Freeware is most often created by a single individual who has an idea to create something, usually for personal use. After the little application is developed, the developer often puts it out on the Internet for anyone and everyone to use. But there's usually a big catch: freeware often comes without documentation, technical support, or even instructions for installing! You're often on your own when it comes to downloading the free flotsam that is scattered over the Web.

Freeware apps also come with large security risks; these applications are often infected with viruses that can damage your files, your operating system, and sometimes even your hardware. Other freeware apps are nothing but digital Trojan horses (called *spyware*). They often come disguised as free little games or "productivity" applications that make your life easier (yeah, right!) If you download and install a freeware app that has spyware embedded inside, you open yourself up to all sorts of trouble. The least damaging spyware tracks the web sites that you visit and reports back to the company that created the software; this information can be sold to other companies that buy lists of prospects who might like their products. The most damaging form of spyware can track things such as passwords and credit cards used for online purchases.

Not all freeware is malicious, but you have to be careful out there when it comes to downloading and installing software on your computer. When it comes to locating freeware, it helps to know a bit more about exactly what you're looking for, and that can often be just as easy as it is difficult. In these instances, I always recommend that you use some of the more trustworthy sites on the Internet that collect, scan, and review freeware. Sites such as `http://appnr.com/` allow you to search for freeware based on category. It still makes sense to investigate any piece of freeware you download (including scanning for viruses), but sites such as this one are often safer than doing a Google search and downloading the first app you find that meets your need.

Are you looking for more freeware download sites for Ubuntu? Try these:

- `http://www.getdeb.net/`

- `http://ubuntulinuxhelp.com/top-100-of-the-best-useful-opensource-applications/`

- `http://lifehacker.com/search/Ubuntu/`

- `http://download.cnet.com/webware-apps/`

- `http://www.sf.net`

What's the Answer?

I now return to the original question posted at the beginning of the chapter: how can you keep expenses down when it comes to software for your U-PC? Now that you're aware of the different types of software and the potential costs with some of them, do what I do and ask yourself two questions: when should I pay for software and when should I look for free software?

The answer to both questions really comes down to a personal choice. I like playing computer games, and many of the game titles I want to play cost money. Yes there are free games, but they're typically not as complex and well-developed as the pay-to-use titles (but sometimes I'm pleasantly surprised by a free game). So, in this case, I don't mind spending money sometimes to get the software I want, especially if there simply isn't a competing product.

But there is a lot of competition for other things I use my computer to do: word processing and photo editing, for example. I don't have $400.00 to drop on the most popular photo editing software, but I've found that Picasa (see Chapter 8) not only provides what I need in a photo editing app but many people (including me) also believe that it's better than the pay-to-use, big name software!

The remaining chapters in this book introduce you to some alternative applications that are applying some competition to the BNAs. Read through the chapters, examine what the software does and how it performs, and ask yourself this question: "Can this application provide me with the features I need?" If the answer is yes, you've taken a good step forward in further reducing your computer expenses.

FREE SOFTWARE WEB SITES

There are a ton of web sites out there that collect free software and allow you to search using keywords and/or categories—a good example is SnapFiles (http://www.snapfiles.com), shown in Figure 3-6. But be careful with these kinds of web sites—what they list as "free" can often mean free to download and install for a period of time. In other words, they offer trialware, and you'll have to pay to keep using it.

One form of free software you'll probably encounter on these sites is *shareware*. This type of software is usually provided on the honor system (you're asked to pay a small fee or make a donation if you like the software and want to continue using it.) I like SnapFiles because it has two tabs in the top-right corner (Freeware and Shareware) that immediately get you to 100 percent free versus trialware/shareware.

Services such as SnapFiles do a good job of filtering out the junk as well as scanning the free stuff for viruses and other malware, but don't always assume that's the case. With any software you download from these types of sites (or anywhere, actually), always run a virus scan to make sure that the installation files are clean.

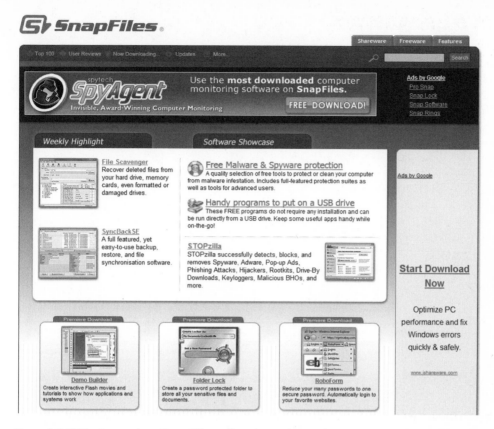

Figure 3-6. *Web sites such as SnapFiles collect free software for visitors to sift through.*

What's Next?

Finally! You're ready to start using some of the great free software that comes bundled with the Ubuntu installation. One reason why the Ubuntu installation is so nice is that because the software is already installed for you, you can immediately start using it and avoid the entire issue of installing and troubleshooting it (e-mail, web browsing, word processing, photo editing, and more). In a couple of instances, however, newer versions of some of the applications exist, and I'll show you how to upgrade to the latest versions in their respective chapters.

Chapter 4 starts with coverage of the 100 percent free, open source, e-mail application called Evolution. And even though I use Google Email 90 percent of the time (see Chapter 10), I do maintain a couple of older e-mail addresses using Evolution. I *love* this application, and I think you'll find it an impressive alternative to the pay-to-use e-mail apps. Let's get started.

E-mail Revolution

I run a variety of applications on my computer, including a word processor, web browser, and music player. But the one application that I seem to use the most is for e-mail. I use e-mail so much that when I went on vacation last year and didn't have Internet access, I think I actually went through e-mail withdrawal for a few days.

Our reliance on e-mail has become as common as phone and television access. Kids these days probably can't imagine that there was a time when e-mail didn't exist. And for some of us aged 25 and older, it's getting hard to remember how we ever got by without it.

I don't think it's an overstatement to say that e-mail has changed our lives. Short of a phone call (or using a chat program for instant messaging), e-mail is the fastest way to communicate with someone next door or on the other side of the planet. Where documents and pictures and other types of files used to have to be mailed in an envelope (at the mercy of the postal service), now these documents are simply included with an e-mail.

Your new U-PC is now installed with Ubuntu (see Chapters 2 and 3). A large number of applications have also been installed on the computer, absolutely free. And tucked nicely into that collection is a superb little e-mail application called Evolution with a list of features that will surprise you.

Evolution Overview

The Evolution application included with the Ubuntu installation runs seamlessly with the operating system and can be minimized on the desktop when you don't need to use it. It uses a simple user interface that is intuitive to grasp, and technical help is just a mouse click away. Evolution is your one-stop shop for the following:

- *E-mail*: Send/receive messages, apply filters, create folders, and identify and block spam

- *Calendar*: Create appointments, set reminders, and invite participants

- *To-do list*: Organize your thoughts and create tasks immediately so you don't forget

- *Contact list*: Maintain e-mail, phone numbers, mailing addresses, and more for your contacts

Like some users, you might find that you only need to send and receive e-mail; if that's the case, the calendar and to-do list sections later in the chapter can be skipped. I do recommend that you read the contact list section, though, because sending e-mail is a lot easier when you don't have to commit someone's address (such as `john.a.smith.jr@traditionalcarsandtrucks.com`) to memory (or the phone number and mailing address).

Similarly, even if you use the web-based e-mail system Google Mail (Gmail, which is covered in Chapter 10), you'll find that Evolution can download your messages and give you access to them even when you're not online. (Gmail supports POP, which allows applications such as Evolution to grab messages and download them to your computer instead of accessing them from a web browser.) Evolution also provides a nice calendar application for your U-PC.

■Note I'm making two assumptions in this chapter. One is that you have an e-mail address that you already use, possibly provided by your Internet Service Provider (ISP), employer, or other entity. If you don't have an e-mail address, contact your ISP; it can provide the steps (or web site) for creating an e-mail address for your personal use.

The second assumption is that you understand basic e-mail terminology: *send*, *receive*, *attachment*, *spam*, and so on. Certain sections of the chapter might go into a little more detail about these subjects, but the purpose of this book isn't to teach you how to use e-mail, but how to use Evolution for e-mail. If you need help on the basics of e-mail, I recommend a visit to `http://communication.howstuffworks.com/email.htm`.

Before you begin using Evolution, you'll have to specify some settings that will allow it to send and receive messages and perform other tasks. If you've installed Ubuntu on your U-PC, you're ready to begin.

Configuring Evolution

The first time you open Evolution, the application detects that it has not yet been configured. A wizard will lead you through the simple process, so follow along with the steps and screenshots, and Evolution will be up and running in no time.

From the Ubuntu desktop, locate and click the Evolution icon, as shown in Figure 4-1.

Figure 4-1. *The Evolution application can be launched quickly using this icon.*

The first time you click this icon, a configuration wizard runs; after Evolution has been configured, you can click this icon to open the application or click Applications ➤ Internet ➤ Evolution Mail (also seen in Figure 4-1). Either method opens the application.

Next, the Evolution Setup Assistant screen appears, as shown in Figure 4-2. Press the Enter key to continue.

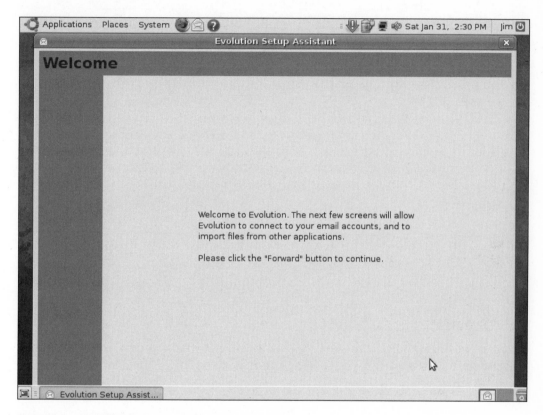

Figure 4-2. *Evolution Setup Assistant opening screen*

■Note Depending on your computer's video resolution, some of the configuration screens might appear large, such as the one shown in Figure 4-2. This can cause some buttons to not appear on the screen (for example, the Forward button mentioned in Figure 4-2). In those instances, hitting the Tab key jumps you to the next button or text field, and pressing Shift+Tab jumps to the previous button or field. In this instance, you can use the reverse jump to select the proper button that might not be visible—in most instances, it is a Next, Continue, or Finished button. This is definitely one of the items that Ubuntu developers have to fix in future versions of the operating system.

The next screen is the "Restore from backup" option seen in Figure 4-3. Because this is the first time you've used Evolution, you'll skip this step. Simply press Enter to move to the next screen.

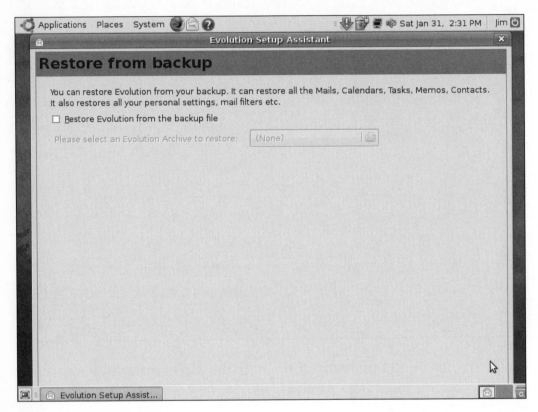

Figure 4-3. *Restoring a backup of your e-mail is an option, but not for this first configuration.*

The next screen is the Identity screen (see Figure 4-4).

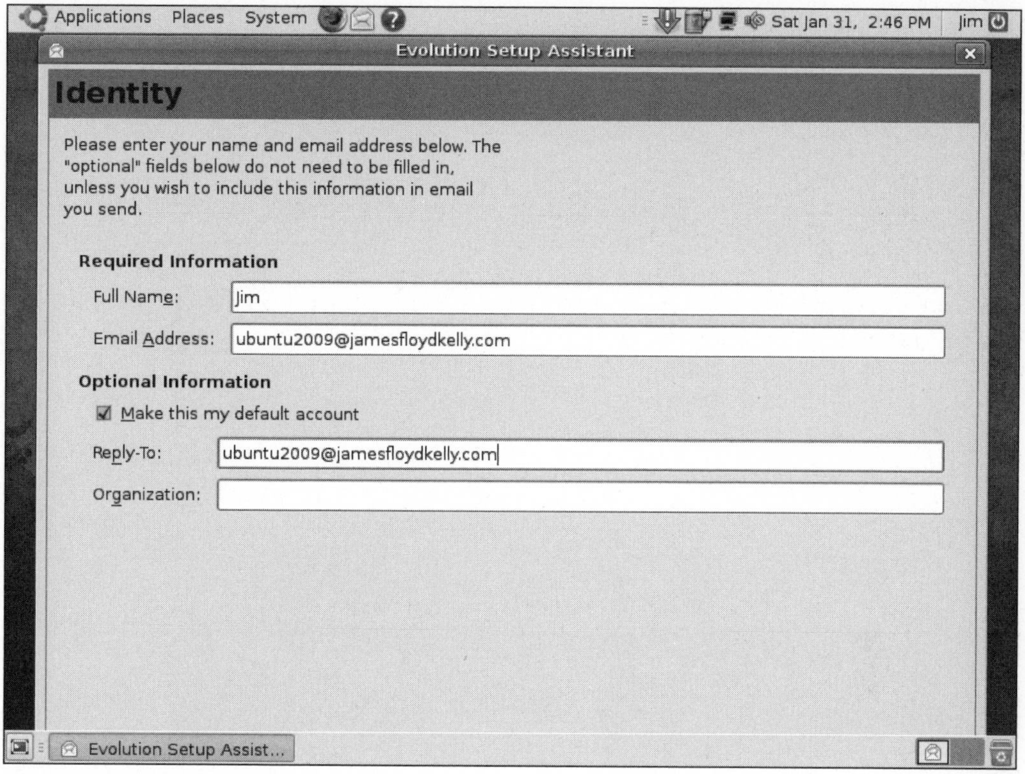

Figure 4-4. *Evolution uses your identity information when you send e-mail.*

For Figure 4-4, enter your e-mail address, leave the box labeled "Make this my default account" checked, and then enter your e-mail address again in the Reply-To field. Click the Forward button (if you can't see the Forward button, press the Tab key four times and then press Enter.)

Evolution won't do you much good unless it can both receive and send e-mail. Figure 4-5 shows the Receiving Email screen, in which you select the type of server that Evolution will use to download your e-mail from the Server Type drop-down menu. If you are uncertain about this, contact your ISP (or other organization that is providing you with an e-mail address) and ask which type to use: POP, IMAP, Microsoft Exchange, or other.

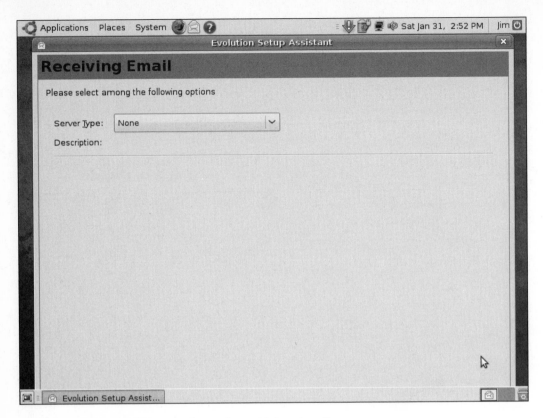

Figure 4-5. *You must select a server type for receiving e-mail.*

Figure 4-6 shows that I selected POP. I also provided a server (pop.secureserver.net, but yours will most likely be different) and my username, which my ISP informs me is simply my username. I don't have to configure the security or authentication items shown in Figure 4-6, but your e-mail provider might require you to use them (configure them based on your provider's instructions).

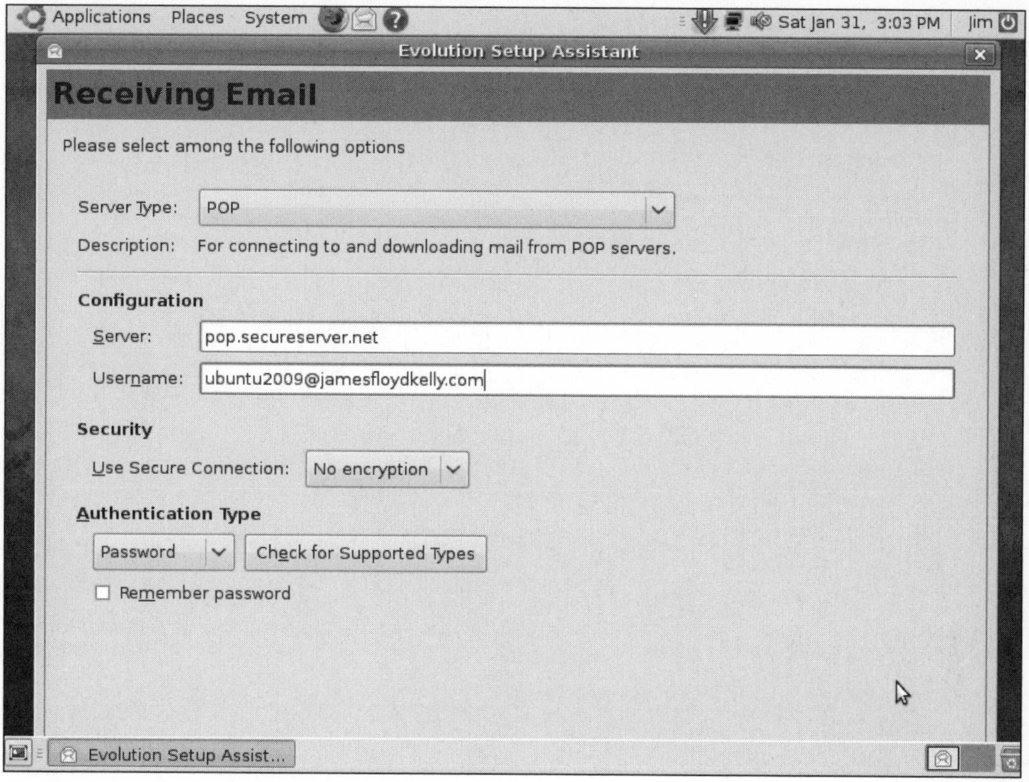

Figure 4-6. *The Receiving Email configuration screen*

■**Note** Again, the information you will use for the screen shown in Figure 4-6 will be slightly different, but 90 percent of the time it will be POP, IMAP, or Exchange Server. Some servers require only a username, not a full e-mail address as I supplied; check with the organization providing your e-mail address for the proper server type and configuration details.

Click the Forward button. (If you cannot see the Forward button, do this: place a check in the box labeled "Remember password" and then uncheck it again. Now press the Tab key three times and press Enter. If the box is already checked, uncheck it and recheck it, press Tab three times, and then press Enter.) Figure 4-7 shows the Receiving Options screen you'll see next.

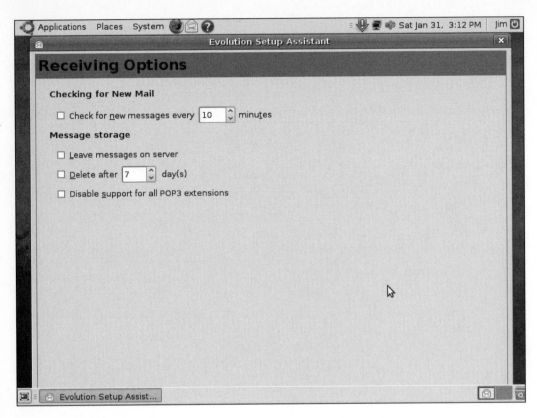

Figure 4-7. *Configure settings for received e-mail on the Receiving Options screen*

You can increase or decrease the time interval for Evolution to check for new messages. The default is 10 minutes and works fine. (I don't recommend decreasing it to anything less than five minutes.) If you place a check in the box labeled "Leave messages on server," copies of every e-mail you receive will be stored remotely until your maximum storage space is reached (in my case, 1GB) or deleted if you check the box labeled "Delete after x day(s)."

Press the Forward button to continue. (If you cannot see the Forward button, place a check in the box labeled "Disable support for all POP3 extensions" and then uncheck it again. Now press the Tab key three times and then press Enter. If the box is already checked, uncheck it and recheck it, press Tab three times, and then press Enter.) Figure 4-8 shows the Sending Email screen you will see next.

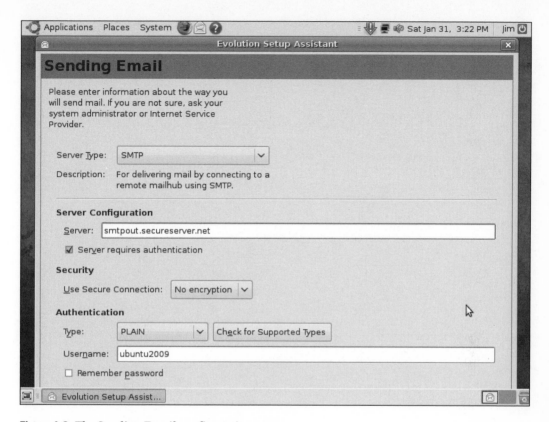

Figure 4-8. *The Sending Email configuration screen*

Once again, you need to determine the server type to use; your options are either SMTP or Sendmail. Most e-mail providers use SMTP, but you should inquire about the proper settings for this window. As you can see, I selected SMTP and provided a name for the Server field.

Click the Forward button to continue. (If you cannot see the Forward button, place a check in the box labeled "Remember password" and then uncheck it again. Now press the Tab key three times and then press Enter. If the box is already checked, uncheck it and recheck it, press Tab three times, and then press Enter.)

Figure 4-9 shows the Account Management screen. You can change the text in the Name field if you like—this screen is useful if you want to have Evolution check multiple e-mail accounts and want to be able to distinguish them easily. I changed my information to Ubuntu-Work as shown in Figure 4-9. Click the Forward button (or press the Tab key three times and press Enter).

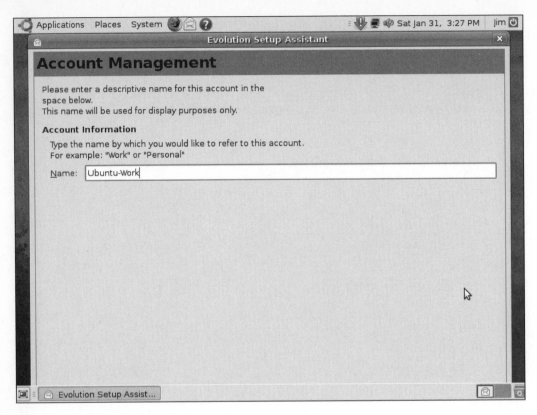

Figure 4-9. *Provide a description in the Account Management screen.*

On the next screen, use your mouse and click the map to indicate your location; your time zone is selected. Click the Forward button (or press the Tab key three times and press Enter).

Figure 4-10 shows the conclusion to the Evolution Setup Assistant. Click the Apply button (or press Enter.)

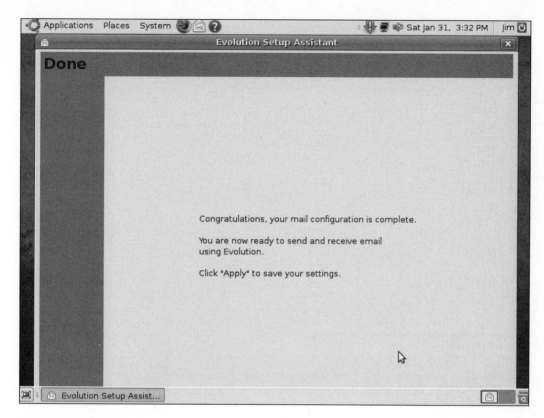

Figure 4-10. *The Evolution Setup Assistant is complete.*

Evolution now opens, as shown in Figure 4-11. The remainder of the chapter will show you how to use all the tools that Evolution provides.

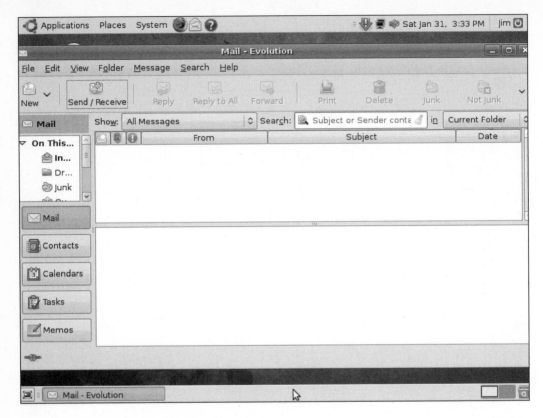

Figure 4-11. *Evolution's user interface is ready to go.*

Using Evolution E-mail

This section shows you how to send and receive e-mail as well as how to send file attachments.

Checking for E-mail

By default, Evolution contacts your e-mail provider every 10 minutes (refer to Figure 4-7) to check for waiting mail to be downloaded. You can choose to manually check for e-mail, no matter the time interval, by clicking the Send/Receive button (refer to Figure 4-11).

When you click the Send/Receive button, you might see a window pop up (similar to the one shown in Figure 4-12). This window asks for the e-mail account password. Enter the password and click the OK button. Until you log off, this password needs to be provided only one time; Evolution remembers the password for subsequent e-mail checks.

■**Note** Back in Figure 4-6, I could have provided the password but I prefer that anyone opening up Evolution not be able to download my mail automatically; feel free to provide your password if you don't want to see this password screen every time.

Figure 4-12. *Evolution requires a password to download e-mail messages.*

You see a screen similar to the one shown in Figure 4-13. Evolution checks with your e-mail provider to see whether any messages are in the queue awaiting download. New messages will appear in the Inbox.

Figure 4-13. *Evolution displays a progress bar while downloading any e-mail messages.*

Unread e-mail appear in your Inbox in bold (refer to Figure 4-11).

Sending E-mail

There are four ways to send e-mail, described in the following sections.

Creating a New Message

Click the New button shown in Figure 4-11. A blank e-mail opens, as shown in Figure 4-14.

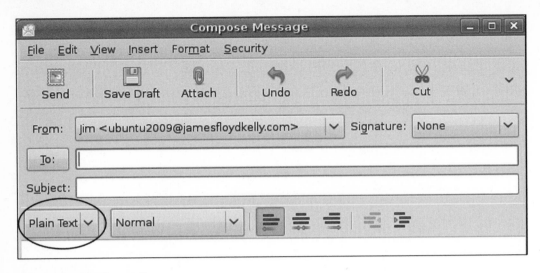

Figure 4-14. *Blank e-mail message*

Enter text in the lower portion of the screen. If you want to apply formatting to the text, select HTML from the drop-down box labeled Plain Text (indicated in Figure 4-14). Selecting HTML provides additional formatting features, as shown in Figure 4-15. Hover your mouse pointer over any of the buttons and a small "hint" balloon appears and describes that button's function.

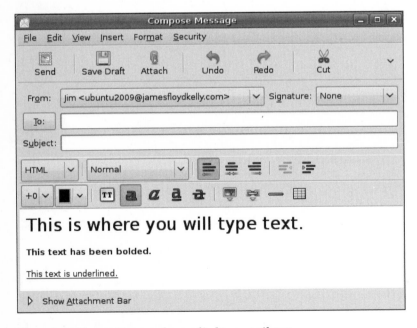

Figure 4-15. *Formatting can be applied to e-mail text.*

To send an attachment (or multiple attachments), click the Attach button shown in Figure 4-15. A The Insert Attachment screen appears (see Figure 4-16).

Tip The technical editor of this book pointed out that you can also drag and drop a file into the message portion of the screen; an attachment is automatically created. If you have a folder open on your screen with the desired file visible, just drag it over to the body of your e-mail and drop it in—easy!

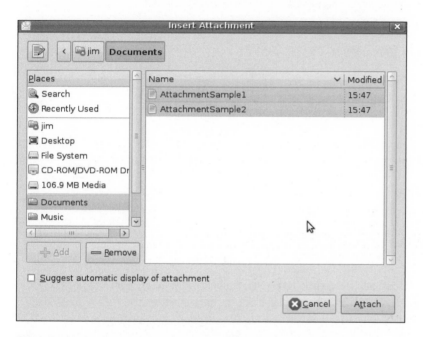

Figure 4-16. *Attachments can be easily added to any message.*

Use the left side of the screen (labeled Places) to browse to the location of the file(s) you want to attach. Select the file from the list on the right side of the screen and click the Attach button. (Multiple files can be selected by holding down the Ctrl key.) In Figure 4-16, I selected two text files, AttachmentSample1 and AttachmentSample2, from the Documents folder. After I click the Attach button, the attachments are shown added to my message at the bottom of the window (see Figure 4-17).

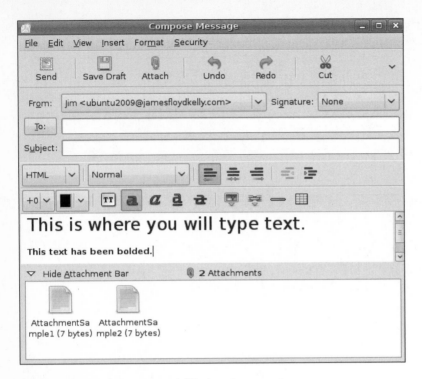

Figure 4-17. *Attachments are visible in your message.*

■**Note** To remove an attachment, simply click it and press the Delete key. To add more attachments, you can use a shortcut; simply right-click any blank portion inside the attachment area and select the "Add attachment" pop-up button.

Finally, you need to specify who will receive the e-mail and add a subject line. I'll cover the contact list later in the chapter, but for now type in your recipient's e-mail address. Use commas to separate multiple e-mail addresses. If you want to add Cc or Bcc lines, click the View menu and select Cc Field and/or Bcc Field; then type in e-mail addresses for those fields. Add some text in the subject line. Figure 4-18 shows the message ready to be sent.

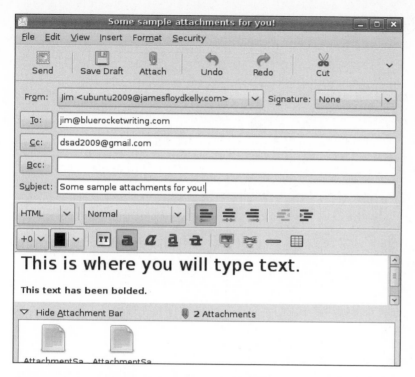

Figure 4-18. *An e-mail with attachments is ready to send.*

Click the Send button shown in Figure 4-18 and your e-mail is sent.

Replying to the Sender of an Existing Message

To reply to an e-mail, open the message by clicking it. The message will open, as shown in Figure 4-19.

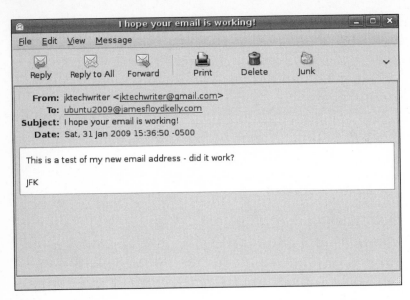

Figure 4-19. *An open e-mail message can be replied to with a click of a button.*

Click the Reply button, and a new e-mail message appears with the text from the original e-mail included at the bottom. Type in your message, as shown in Figure 4-20, and click the Send button. You can change the subject line, add attachments, or delete the original message text. You can also treat it just like a new message, including adding formatting (as described in the previous section).

Replying to All Recipients of a Particular Message

Just like replying to a single recipient, clicking the Reply to All button shown in Figure 4-19 will allow you to respond to an e-mail and send a response to all the addresses in the To and Cc fields of the original message. Your response will not be sent to anyone included in the Bcc field of the original message.

You can format text, add attachments, and even add new e-mail addresses to the Reply to All message. (You can also delete e-mail addresses in a Reply to All message, but it's often considered bad etiquette.)

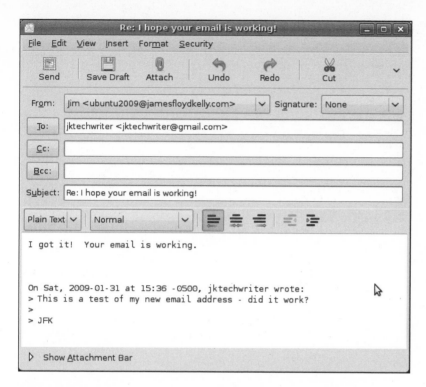

Figure 4-20. *A reply to this message includes the original message text.*

Forwarding an Existing Message

You can also choose to forward an open e-mail message to a new recipient; maybe you received an interesting web site link or an attachment that you want to share with someone else. All that's required is to click the Forward button (refer to Figure 4-19). You'll need to provide at least one e-mail address; click the Send button when done, and the e-mail will be forwarded to the new recipient(s).

ADDITIONAL E-MAIL OPTIONS

In addition to sending and receiving message, you can also perform the following tasks:

- *Print a message*: Select an e-mail in your Inbox (or double-click one to open it) and click the Print button.

- *Identify spam*: From the Inbox, click a spam message once and then click the Junk button. Your message will be removed to the junk folder.

- *Create new folders*: Click the Folder menu and select the New option. Give your folder a name, specify where to store it (possibly as a subfolder of the Inbox), and click Create.

- *Search for messages*: If you're looking for a specific e-mail but have hundreds or thousands to sift through, click the Search menu and select the Advanced Search option. Provide keywords that you want to search for and click the OK button; any messages that contain one or more keywords will be listed onscreen.

- *Open attachments*: If you receive an e-mail attachment, simply double-click the attachment, and that file's default application will open the file. For example, double-clicking an attachment labeled `recipes.odt` will open the document using OpenOffice Writer (covered in Chapter 5). The `.odt` file extension is the default OpenOffice Writer file type, but it can also be used to open `.doc` files as well.

Using Evolution Calendar and Tasks

Evolution provides an easy-to-use calendar and the ability to create a list of tasks (a to-do list). To access the Calendar and Tasks features, click the Calendars button in the lower-left corner, as shown in Figure 4-21.

Figure 4-21. *Accessing the Evolution calendar is a button click away.*

Figure 4-22 shows the default Calendar and Tasks window open. Tasks is located at the right edge of the screen, and Calendar takes up the middle and left sections. (Note that you can switch back to Evolution Mail by clicking the Mail button in the lower-left corner.)

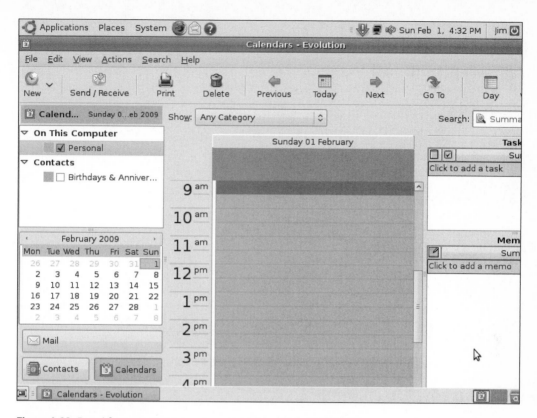

Figure 4-22. *Provide a username and password to log in to Ubuntu.*

Let's start by creating a task. In the upper-right corner of Figure 4-22 you'll see a line of text that says "Click to add a task." Click that bit of text and type in something short and sweet that you need to accomplish. Feel free to type in as many tasks as you want; as the list builds up, you can scroll up and down the list. As your task list builds, you can place checks in boxes to indicate that certain tasks are complete. The Tasks feature is simply a nice visual reminder for you when you're working in Evolution. Figure 4-23 shows that I've got some work ahead of me. (To remove an item from the task list, right-click it and select Delete.)

Figure 4-23. *Use the Tasks feature to give yourself friendly reminders.*

In the lower-right corner of Figure 4-22 you'll see another bit of text that says "Click to add a memo." Memos don't come with check boxes and they give you a bit more space to type. Memos are also specific to a certain day on your calendar; tasks are always visible, but memos appear only on the day they are assigned (more on that later). Figure 4-24 shows a few memos I've written; by right-clicking a memo, the text can be copied and pasted into an e-mail or document of your choice.

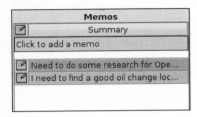

Figure 4-24. *Memos are useful for storing longer bits of text.*

■**Note** Memos and tasks are really useful when you assign a date to them by using the calendar (I'll show you how to do that shortly). Just remember that tasks are for short reminders, and memos are for adding comments and notes and then applying them to specific days on your calendar. Memos are better than tasks for typing longer bits of text for later use in other documents or tools.

Now let's focus on using the Calendar feature. Figure 4-25 shows a minicalendar that displays a full month. You can use the small arrows to the left and right of the month and year to move forward and backward to the month/year you want to view. The current date is indicated by a small square surrounding the date (February 1, 2009 in Figure 4-25), and other days you select are highlighted by a solid-colored square.

‹	February 2009					›
Mon	Tue	Wed	Thu	Fri	Sat	Sun
26	27	28	29	30	31	1
2	3	4	5	6	7	8
9	10	11	12	13	14	15
16	17	18	19	20	21	22
23	24	25	26	27	28	1
2	3	4	5	6	7	8

Figure 4-25. *The minicalendar lets you select a specific day to add or view activities.*

Clicking a particular day one time shows you a list of that day's activities in one-hour increments, as shown in Figure 4-26. In this example, I clicked February 14, 2009 and scrolled down the activity list to view my evening schedule.

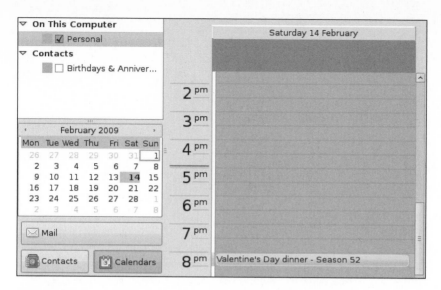

Figure 4-26. *The calendar shows my dinner plans for the evening.*

Although I check my calendar constantly, sometimes I want to set a reminder to alert me in advance. To do this, I double-click the event. A screen like the one in Figure 4-27 appears.

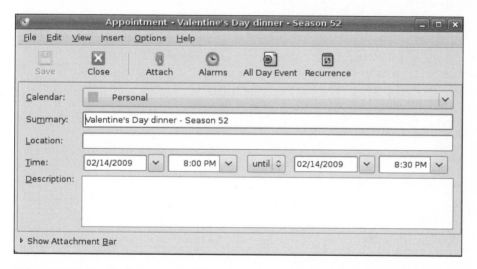

Figure 4-27. *Calendar lets you configure alerts to remind you of appointments.*

To configure a reminder, click the Alarms button shown in Figure 4-27. Figure 4-28 shows you the alarm configuration screen that appears.

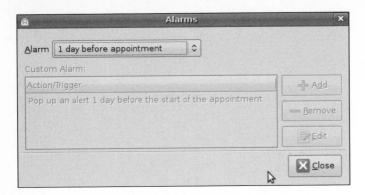

Figure 4-28. *The alarm configuration screen*

Click the Alarm drop-down menu and select an appropriate reminder time. In this example, I elected to be reminded one day prior to the appointment. Click the Close button when done, and the appointment will now have a small icon indicating that an alarm has been set (see Figure 4-29).

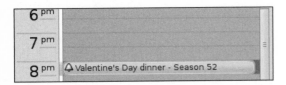

Figure 4-29. *An alarm icon indicates that an appointment reminder has been created.*

On February 13, 2009, when I opened Evolution, I saw a small alert open in the lower-right corner of the screen similar to the one in Figure 4-30.

Figure 4-30. *Pop-up alerts keep you from forgetting important appointments.*

You can also select different views of your calendar instead of a single day's hourly breakdown. In the upper-right corner of the screen, click the button with the arrow pointing downward (as shown in Figure 4-31), and you can choose three additional views for your calendar: Week, Month, or List. In this example, I selected the Month view. (Click the Day button, also shown in Figure 4-31, to return to the standard Day view seen in Figure 4-26.)

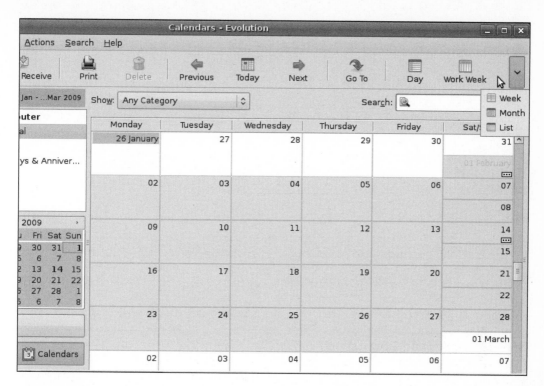

Figure 4-31. *Change how your calendar appears (this is the Month view).*

To create a new appointment (in any view: Day, Week, Month, List), double-click the view. Depending on your view, you see a screen similar to the one shown in Figure 4-32. In Day view, for example, double-clicking 6pm fills in the time of the new appointment; double-clicking February 14 in Month view likewise fills in the day of the appointment, but not the time. Click the Save button when done, and your appointment is added to your calendar.

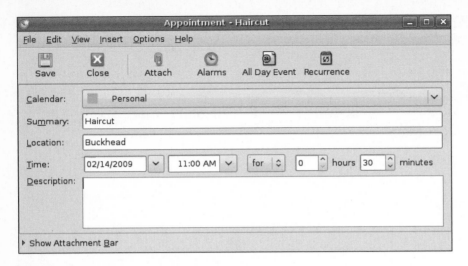

Figure 4-32. *Create a new calendar appointment.*

Calendar has many more features, including printing out a day's, week's, or month's worth of activities. You can have your contact list (which is covered in the next section) automatically add your friends' and colleagues' birthdays to your calendar. The View menu lets you toggle between full-screen views of Tasks, Memos, and Calendar. And the Search menu lets you do a keyword search of all your appointments and provides a list of all appointments that satisfy the search requirements.

Using Evolution Contacts

The last feature of Evolution discussed here is Contacts. Because Contacts is built into Evolution, it can be used with both the Calendar and Email tools. For example, if you add your best friend's contact information to the list, including phone number, birthday, mailing address, and e-mail address, you can click the To button (refer to Figure 4-15) and select his name instead of typing his full e-mail address. Calendar can also be configured to display all your contacts' birthdays—if you launch Evolution every day to check your e-mail and calendar, you'll never have to worry about forgetting to call your buddy on his birthday!

To open up Contacts, click the Contacts button shown in Figure 4-21. The Contacts list opens, as shown in Figure 4-33.

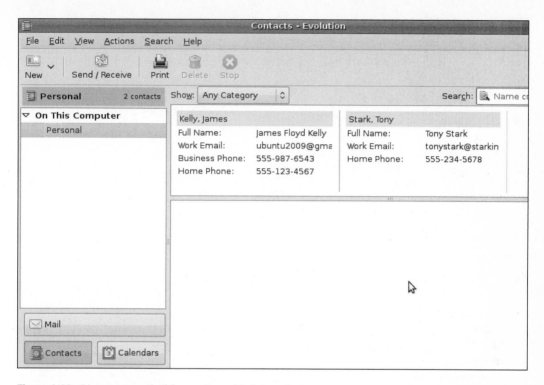

Figure 4-33. *Contacts can hold a variety of information.*

To add a new contact, click the New button shown in Figure 4-33, and a window opens (see Figure 4-34). Fill in as much information as you like and press Enter when done.

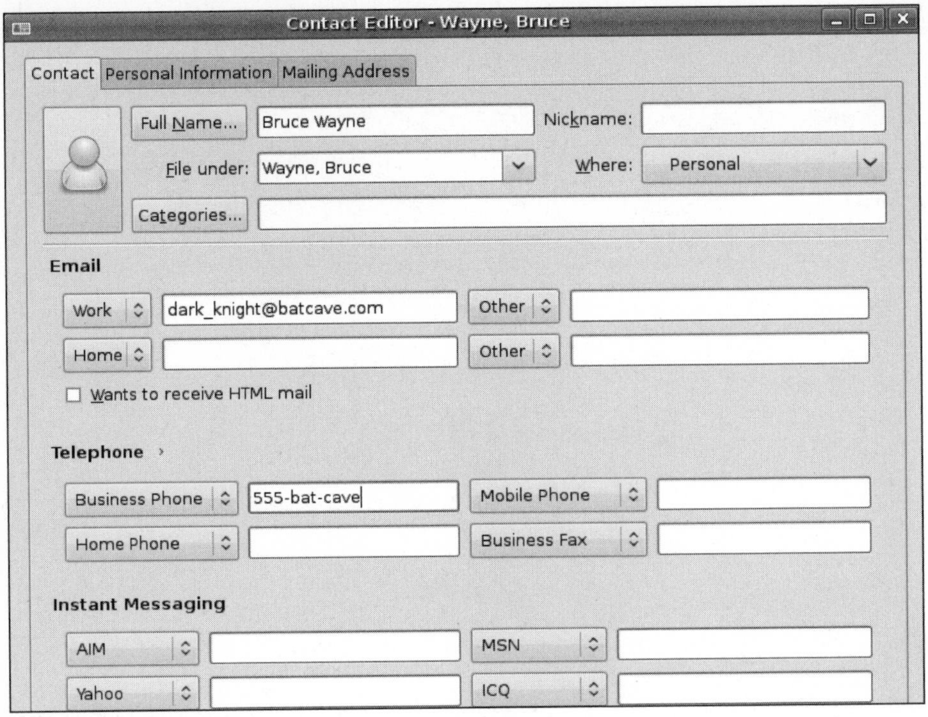

Figure 4-34. *Provide information such as phone number and e-mail address for a contact.*

The information is added to your contact list, as shown in Figure 4-35. Your contacts are listed alphabetically, and e-mail and phone numbers are provided; clicking a contact one time displays additional information at the bottom of the screen. Double-click a contact to add new information.

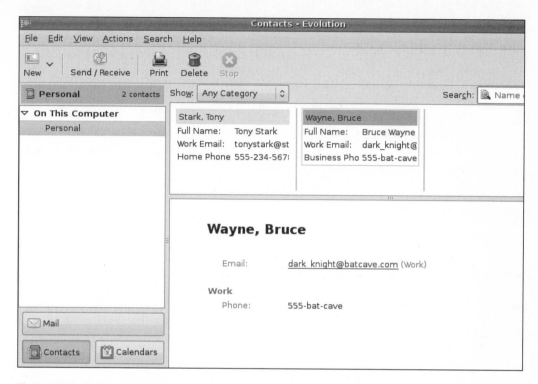

Figure 4-35. *Click a contact to view information at the bottom of the screen.*

If you want to e-mail a contact, simply click the e-mail address; a new e-mail message window appears (similar to the one shown in Figure 4-14), and the contact's e-mail address is automatically added to the To field.

Selecting contacts enables you to print their information by clicking the Print button along the top edge of the Evolution application (refer to Figure 4-35). Likewise, selecting a contact and clicking the Delete button deletes that contact from your list (after selecting Delete from a confirmation warning window that opens).

Summarizing Evolution

There is a lot more to learn about Evolution than I can teach you in this chapter. Evolution comes with a nice Help Wizard that can be launched by clicking the Help menu and selecting Contents and examining the instructions included there. You can also select the Get Help Online option from the Help menu and post questions on the Internet site that opens, as well as search existing questions.

Evolution is an application that resides on your hard drive. This means that your e-mail, calendar, and contacts can be accessed only when you're sitting at your computer. For most people, this isn't an issue, but if you want to be able to access your e-mail, calendar, and contacts from any computer, take a look at Chapter 10, which covers Google's e-mail and calendar tools. After reading that chapter and possibly trying those tools, you'll probably want to choose to use either Evolution or the Google tools, not both (although that's completely possible).

Additional information on Evolution can be found on its official web site; point your web browser to `http://projects.gnome.org/evolution/` for additional information and more discussion about some of the features of Evolution not covered here.

What's Next?

Next in Chapter 5, I'll introduce you to one of the most powerful and popular Open Source applications available: OpenOffice Writer. Writer is a word processor in the same family as big-name applications such as Microsoft Word or Corel WordPerfect, but without a big name price. It's 100 percent free, and I think you'll find that it's a worthy application that can provide the features you'll need in a word processor. Did I mention that it's free?

So, close down Evolution for now or just minimize it to the desktop, and get ready to see what your U-PC can do when it comes to word processing.

CHAPTER 5

Word Processing with Writer

One of the most surprising and welcome applications to see the light of day has to be OpenOffice Writer, one of a handful of applications that comes with the free, open source OpenOffice suite. This powerful word processor is providing some serious competition for the best-selling Microsoft Word.

Microsoft Word is sold as a standalone application (for about $300.00) or bundled in the Microsoft Office suite (starting at about $400.00). Considering that Microsoft Office applications update about every three to four years, the updates can become a large expenditure for a consumer who wants to keep up with the latest and greatest versions.

So, it's a nice change of pace to find a suite of productivity applications (word processor, spreadsheet, and slideshow/presentation software, among others) that is not only packed with features but is also 100 percent free to download, install, and use—no strings attached. The OpenOffice suite of applications is making waves in both the business world and in the home PC market, providing users with a great-looking collection of tools that provide professional-grade results.

In this chapter, I introduce you to OpenOffice Writer, one of three OpenOffice apps covered in the book. (Chapter 6 will cover OpenOffice Calc, a spreadsheet app; Chapter 7 will cover OpenOffice Impress, a slideshow/presentation app.)

OpenOffice Versions for Ubuntu

When you install the Ubuntu operating system (version 8.10 for this book) on your computer, a large collection of free applications is installed, including OpenOffice Writer, Calc, and Impress. The applications are ready to use; no installation required. But the OpenOffice suite has one drawback: the version of OpenOffice installed with the Ubuntu operating system is version 2.4, and the most current version of OpenOffice is version 3.0 (as this chapter is being written).

This chapter uses the version 3.0 user interface for all OpenOffice applications, but there is nothing stopping you from following along with this chapter's examples (as well as those in Chapter 6 and Chapter 7) using version 2.4. There might be slight differences in naming conventions for menus, tool buttons, and windows that open, but many of the actions required while using Writer version 2.4 are similar if not identical to those in version 3.0. That said, I'll provide a web site that contains instructions for upgrading version 2.4 to version 3.0. The upgrade is extremely simple to perform, and the instructions also provide screenshots of the steps for you to follow.

Because OpenOffice version 2.4 already resides on your computer, all that's really needed to upgrade it to version 3.0 is to install a set of files that upgrade the older version, bypassing a full installation of OpenOffice. Here are the steps to do this.

Open your web browser to `http://news.softpedia.com/news/How-To-Install-OpenOffice-org-3-0-in-Ubuntu-8-10-96449.shtml`, as shown in Figure 5-1.

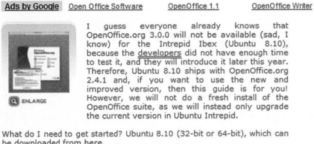

How to Install OpenOffice.org 3.0 on Ubuntu 8.10
Step by step tutorial with screenshots!

Ads by Google   Open Office Software   OpenOffice 1.1   OpenOffice Writer   Cheap Windows Server   Ubuntu ATI

I guess everyone already knows that OpenOffice.org 3.0.0 will not be available (sad, I know) for the Intrepid Ibex (Ubuntu 8.10), because the developers did not have enough time to test it, and they will introduce it later this year. Therefore, Ubuntu 8.10 ships with OpenOffice.org 2.4.1 and, if you want to use the new and improved version, then this guide is for you! However, we will not do a fresh install of the OpenOffice suite, as we will instead only upgrade the current version in Ubuntu Intrepid.

What do I need to get started? Ubuntu 8.10 (32-bit or 64-bit), which can be downloaded from here.

OK, so... first thing, you must add the OpenOffice.org 3.0 repositories, then upgrade the installed packages. Follow the steps below!

STEP 1 - Add the OpenOffice.org 3 repositories

Go to *System -> Administration -> Software Sources...*

Figure 5-1. *Instructions for upgrading to OpenOffice version 3.0 are easy to follow.*

Follow the steps provided on the web site, but be aware that after selecting Software Sources (shown in Figure 5-1), you might see a window that asks for your administrator password (see Figure 5-2). If this window opens, enter your password and click OK.

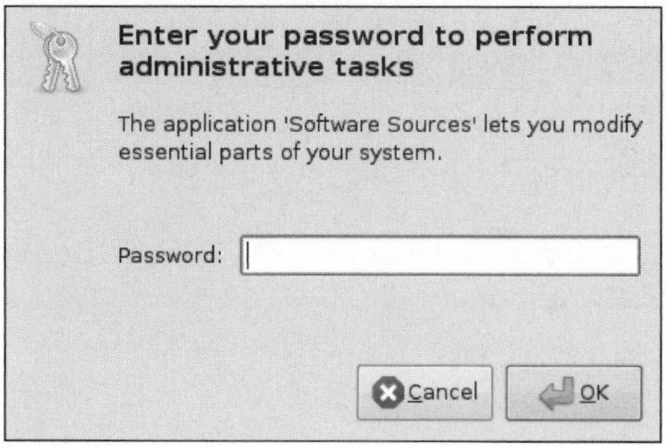

Enter your password to perform administrative tasks

The application 'Software Sources' lets you modify essential parts of your system.

Password: [   ]

⊗ Cancel   ↵ OK

Figure 5-2. *Provide the administrator password if requested.*

Perform the remaining steps described to complete the upgrade. When you finish, all three OpenOffice applications—Writer, Calc, and Impress—will be version 3.0.

Welcome to Writer

Opening OpenOffice Writer couldn't be easier: click the Applications menu, select the Office group, and then click OpenOffice.org Word Processor, as shown in Figure 5-3.

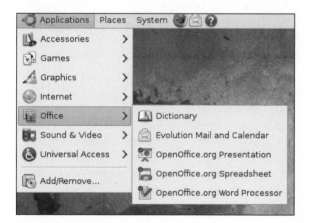

Figure 5-3. *Selecting OpenOffice.org Word Processor opens Writer.*

OpenOffice Writer 3.0 opens in a new window, as shown in Figure 5-4.

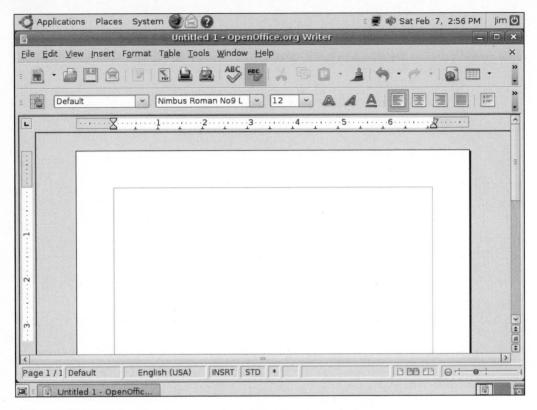

Figure 5-4. *OpenOffice Writer's user interface and a blank document.*

Writer has the typical collection of drop-down menus along the top of the screen: File, Edit, Insert, Format, Table, Tools, Window, and Help. And just below the menu bar is the first of two toolbars. Figure 5-5 shows the first toolbar with some descriptions of some of the buttons. As with many applications, hovering your mouse pointer over a button causes a small tooltip window to appear that can often help you figure out a button's function. You'll also see in Figure 5-5 that clicking the small downward-pointing triangle on the far-right edge of the toolbar opens up additional buttons and tools (along with descriptions).

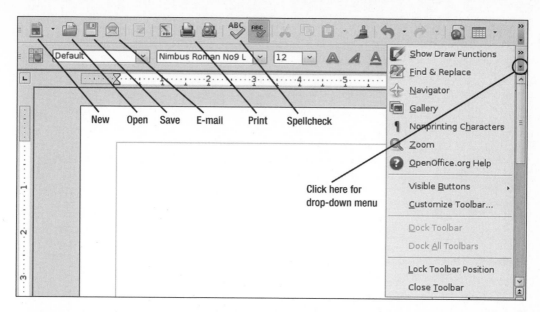

Figure 5-5. *The first toolbar has many options, including print and spellcheck capabilities.*

Figure 5-6 shows the second toolbar along with some descriptions. Notice that a second menu of additional tools is available on this toolbar by clicking the downward-pointing arrow indicated in the figure.

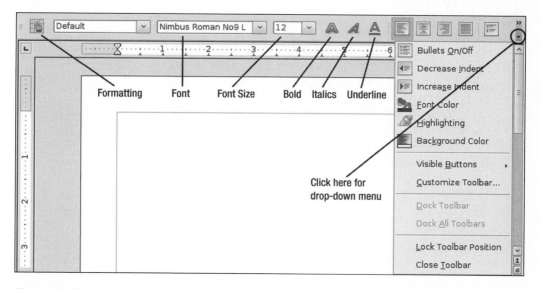

Figure 5-6. *The second toolbar has options for modifying the text in a document.*

Along the bottom edge of Writer is another toolbar, as shown in Figure 5-7. One of the more useful features on this toolbar is the slider in the right corner that allows you to zoom in and out of your document.

Number of Pages   Multiple Page View   Zoom

Figure 5-7. *The bottom toolbar offers the ability to zoom in and out.*

Finally, controls in the upper-right corner of the application allow you to minimize, maximize, and close the window, as indicated in Figure 5-8.

Figure 5-8. *Minimize, maximize, or close the Writer window.*

Throughout the remainder of this chapter, I'll be using these menus, buttons, and tools to demonstrate some of the features and uses of Writer. I encourage you to open Writer and follow along. And as with many applications, I highly encourage you to click the File menu and select the Save option frequently to prevent any loss of work. Now, let's see what you can do with Writer.

Using Writer

In this section, I'm making some basic assumptions about your previous word processing experience. I assume that you know how to enter text, how to select text for formatting, and how to click menus and save files. If you're completely new to word processing (and possibly to using a computer), I recommend that you spend some time inside the OpenOffice Writer Help Center. Click the OpenOffice.org Help option.

When the OpenOffice.org Help window opens (see Figure 5-9), click Instructions for Using OpenOffice.org Writer to learn about the basics of using this word processor. More than 100 basic skills are covered here, including using the mouse pointer to select and format text, indenting paragraphs, setting tabs, adding graphics, and more.

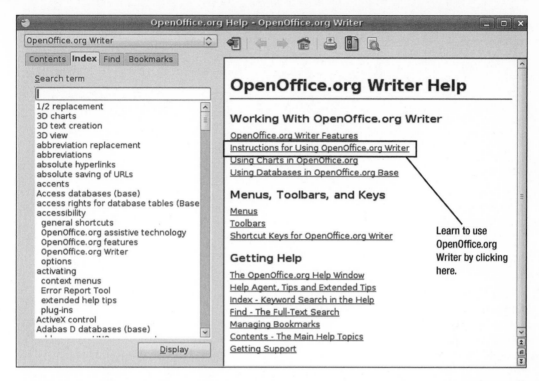

Figure 5-9. *OpenOffice.org Writer Help is a perfect place to learn about basic word processing.*

In the following sections, I'll show you some basic and advanced tasks that you can perform using Writer. For more details on these steps, consult the Help Wizard shown in Figure 5-9.

Fixing Misspelled Words

If you're like me, you can't type a paragraph without a misspelled word creeping into a sentence or two. For me, it's not a reflection of my spelling abilities; I type so fast that I tend to make a lot of mistakes. So it's nice to see that Writer alerts me to my misspelled words by placing a wavy line underneath the problem words, as shown in Figure 5-10.

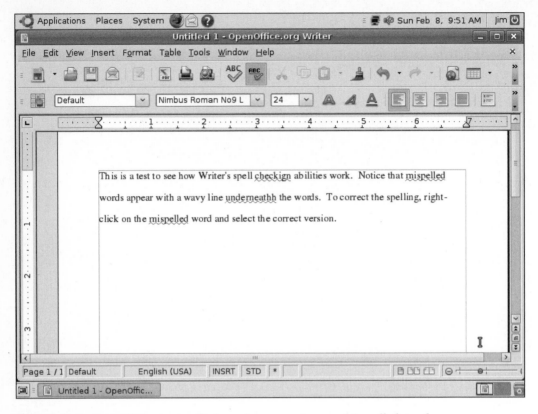

Figure 5-10. *Look at all those mispelled words . . . oops, I mean misspelled words.*

Writer makes it so easy to fix misspelled words, too; simply right-click a misspelled word and select the correctly spelled word, as shown in Figure 5-11. Only a single occurrence of that word is fixed at a time in your document; in Figure 5-10, for example, the incorrectly spelled word *mispelled* appears twice and fixing one of them does not correct the other occurrence.

■**Note** Some might consider this to be a bug, but I need the word *mispelled* to be uncorrected in the previous paragraph and in this sentence. If I corrected the word anywhere else in this document, and the default was to fix all errors of the same word, these two intentional errors would also be fixed—and I don't want that to happen.

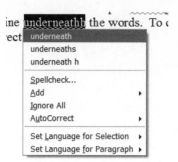

Figure 5-11. *Right-click a misspelled word; suggested fixes are at the top of the list.*

Saving a Document in Different Formats

You can save a document by clicking File ➤ Save. The Save window appears; click the small arrow to the left of "File type" and you'll see a list of file extensions, as shown in Figure 5-12.

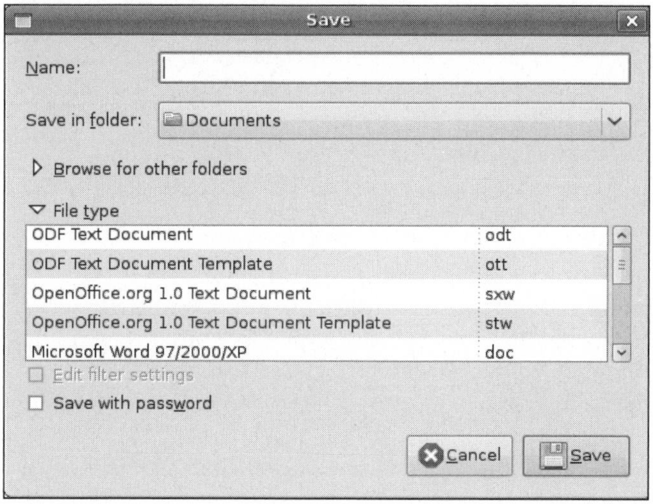

Figure 5-12. *Writer can save documents in many different formats.*

By default, Writer saves your documents using the .odt file type. Scrolling down that list, you'll also see that you can save in .doc format (for compatibility with Microsoft Word) as well as many other formats, including .html (for use as web pages). But you won't find another popular file format, .pdf, in that list. Instead of saving a document as a .pdf file, you must instead export the document as a separate file. To do this, click the PDF button indicated in Figure 5-13; provide a name and location to save the file and then click the Save button. The current document is exported and saved with the .pdf extension.

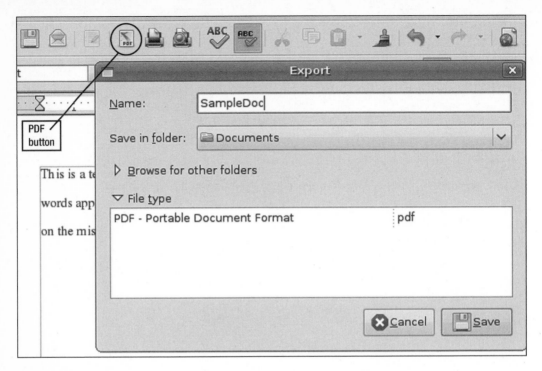

Figure 5-13. *Exporting your file to a .pdf file is as easy as clicking this button.*

Inserting a Picture

Adding a picture to your document is fairly straightforward. Click the Insert menu, click the Picture option, and then select From File on the flyout menu shown in Figure 5-14.

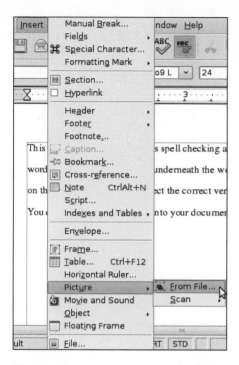

Figure 5-14. *Insert a picture from a file stored on your computer.*

Browse to the location of the desired image, select it, and click the Open button. Your picture is inserted into the document, as shown in Figure 5-15. You can use the small boxes at the corners of the figure to resize the image: click a box and, while holding down the mouse button, drag the mouse in or out to shrink or enlarge the image; release the mouse button when you're done.

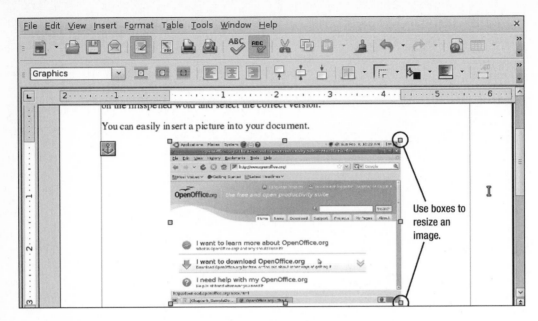

Figure 5-15. *Pictures can be inserted into a document and resized.*

Printing Envelopes

One nice feature that Writer supports is the ability to print envelopes if your printer supports this function. To print an envelope, first load your printer with a blank envelope; consult your printer's documentation for proper orientation and insertion of an envelope.

Next, open a new Writer document, click the Insert menu, and choose the Envelope option. A window opens, in which you can type your address in the Sender box and the recipient's address in the Addressee box (see Figure 5-16).

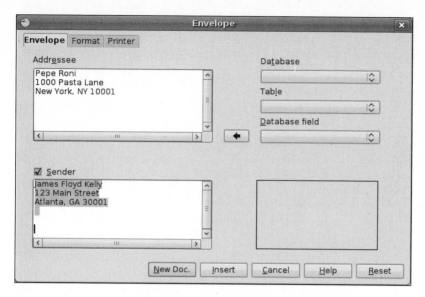

Figure 5-16. *Enter the addresses to be printed on the envelope.*

Next, click the Printer tab, as shown in Figure 5-17, and select the orientation that matches the envelope in the printer. Click the Insert button when you're done.

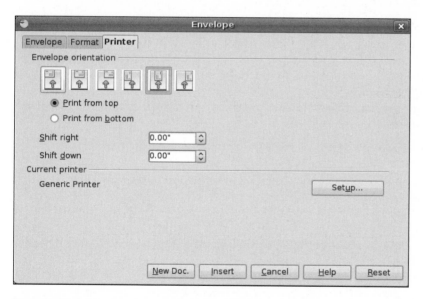

Figure 5-17. *Select the proper envelope orientation for your printer.*

The address information is inserted into the document and can be printed using the Print button, as shown in Figure 5-18.

■Note The Format tab (refer to Figure 5-16) enables you to tweak the placement of the addresses, moving them in or out as well as up and down. Use this option if you don't like Writer's default location for printing the addresses.

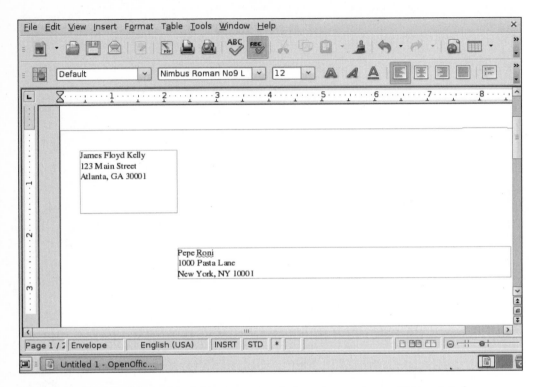

Figure 5-18. *The envelope preview shows you exactly how the envelope will be printed.*

Verify the spelling and placement and then click the Print button; your envelope is printed and ready for a stamp.

PERFORMING A MAIL MERGE

Imagine for a moment that you have a list of 30 people to whom you want to send an important letter. The letter will contain some standard text, but you also want to include some customized content, including the recipient's address, the first name in the greeting, and some other details specific to that person. You could type up the letter, enter the first person's information, print the letter, and then edit the document by removing the first person's information and then adding in the next person, but that process could take a while. Fortunately, OpenOffice Writer provides a better way: a *mail merge*.

A mail merge pulls custom information from a database or spreadsheet application and then inserts that information into a word processing document. Where that information is placed is determined by you; you create the basic format of the letter and then specify placeholders in which the custom information will be inserted.

The instructions for using the mail merge feature aren't difficult, but the number of steps is extensive, and the process involves using two applications: both OpenOffice.org Writer and OpenOffice.org Calc. OpenOffice.org has created an easy-to-follow .pdf file that you can download that walks you through the entire process for performing a mail merge. The document can be downloaded from http://documentation.openoffice.org/manuals/userguide3/0211WG3-UsingMailMerge.pdf.

Printing Labels

You can purchase precut labels for your printer and use Writer to insert your text on the labels before printing. Click the File menu, select New, and then choose Labels. The window shown in Figure 5-19 appears.

Select the label brand from the Brand drop-down list shown in Figure 5-19. Avery is a popular label type, and I selected the 5260 Address labels from the Type drop-down list.

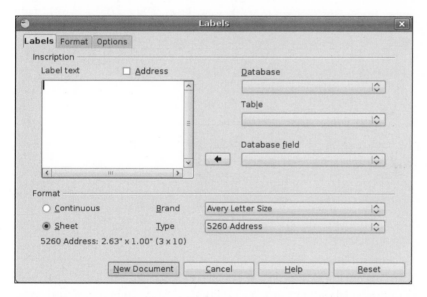

Figure 5-19. *Select the label brand and type to create a custom label sheet.*

Click the New Document button, and a preconfigured label template is created like the one shown in Figure 5-20.

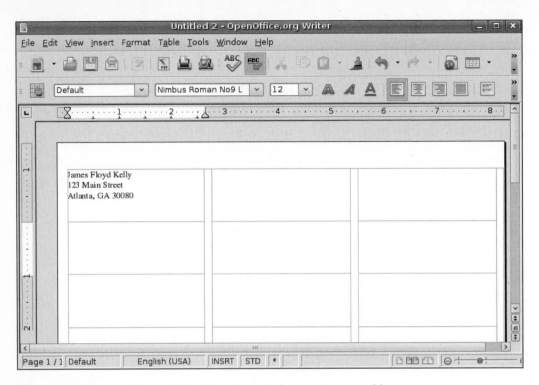

Figure 5-20. *The preconfigured label sheet is ready for you to enter addresses.*

Note If you can't find your exact label type, click the Format tab (refer to Figure 5-19) to create a custom label sheet; this requires you to provide some measurements of your label sheet.

Inserting Special Characters

Sometimes you need to add a unique character to your document; foreign currency symbols are a good example. Place the cursor where you want to insert the special character, click the Insert menu, and select the Special Character option. The Special Characters window opens, as shown in Figure 5-21.

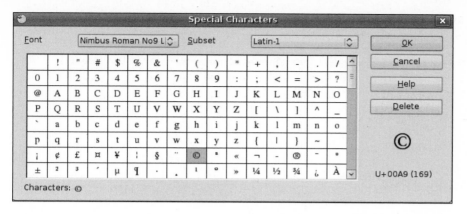

Figure 5-21. *Use the Special Characters tool to find nonstandard text and symbols.*

Select a font and scroll through the window to find the desired character. Click the OK button, and the special character is inserted into the document (see Figure 5-22).

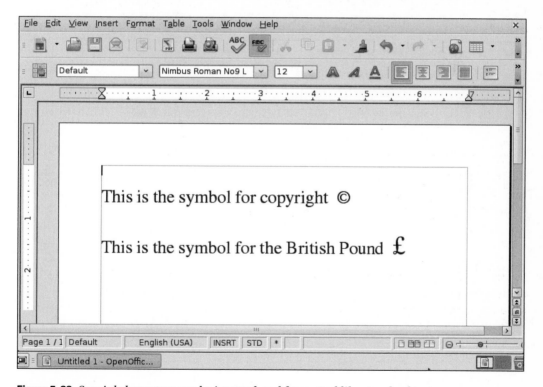

Figure 5-22. *Special characters can be inserted and formatted like standard text.*

Preventing Changes to Text

If you create a document to share with other users but want to protect a small (or large) portion of the text from being changed or deleted, Writer allows you to lock a portion of text with a password; only someone with the password can then make changes.

Highlight the text you want to protect, as shown in Figure 5-23.

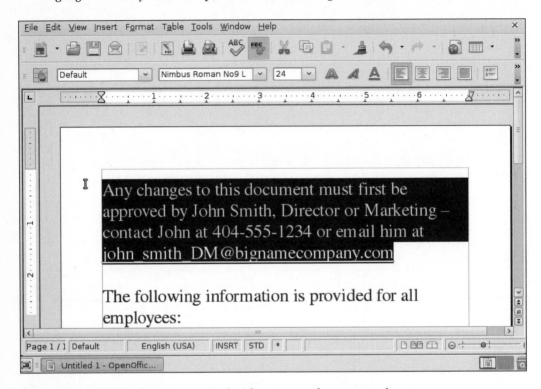

Figure 5-23. *Highlighted text is protected with a password to prevent changes.*

Click the Insert menu and select the Section option. The window shown in Figure 5-24 opens; place a check in the box labeled Protect and select the box labeled "With password." Provide a password in the window that appears; retype the password and click OK to return to the screen shown in Figure 5-23. Click the Insert button, and the text is locked.

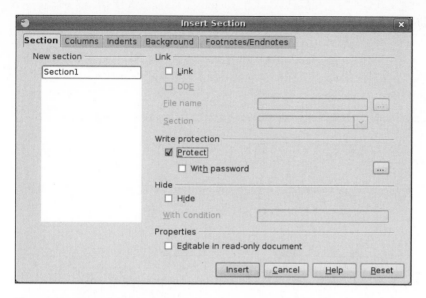

Figure 5-24. *Provide a password to protect and lock selected text.*

Any attempted changes to the locked text result in a warning message similar to the one shown in Figure 5-25.

Figure 5-25. *Attempts to modify locked text result in a warning message.*

Summarizing Writer

Writer is a full-featured word processing application with the ability to save documents in a variety of standard and popular formats such as .odt, .doc, .html, and .pdf. Users of other word processing applications can open, read, print, and edit documents created in Writer without any concerns about compatibility.

Users can also count on reliable technical support from a community of OpenOffice users, including many of the application developers as well as typical day-to-day users who are willing to help others with questions. One of the best sources of help and information on OpenOffice Writer (as well as Calc and Impress—covered in Chapters 6 and 7) is the official OpenOffice web forum found at http://user.services.openoffice.org/en/forum/. You can search the extensive database of existing questions and answers, and post your own questions. Figure 5-26 shows that each OpenOffice application has its own category, with Writer being at the top of the list—followed by Calc, Impress, and more.

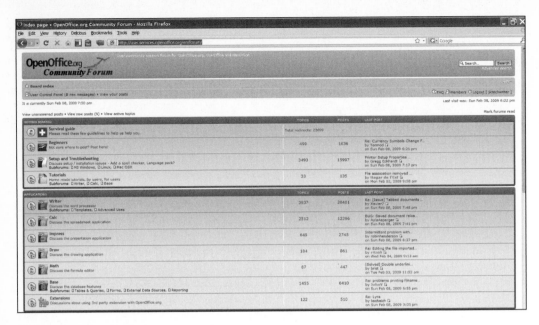

Figure 5-26. *The OpenOffice.org Community Forum*

In addition to the forum, the OpenOffice Wiki at `http://wiki.services.openoffice.org/wiki/Main_Page` is another great source of tutorials and information. Unlike the forum, questions aren't posted here, but the OpenOffice community of users continually updates the Wiki with frequently asked questions (FAQs) and how-to articles that you can print out or follow along with as you use an application.

Tip If you're really interested in learning OpenOffice.org 3.0, check out the new book, *Beginning OpenOffice 3*, by Andy Channelle (Apress); you'll find every nook and cranny of OpenOffice.org covered in this great resource.

What's Next?

Chapter 6 will examine the OpenOffice spreadsheet application called Calc. You'll see examples of many of the spreadsheet functions available via Calc as well as how to add spreadsheet information to a document created with Writer. So let's move ahead to the next OpenOffice application and see how it works with the Ubuntu operating system.

Spreadsheets with Calc

Spreadsheets aren't just for accountants. I have a friend who uses spreadsheets to track his fantasy football team's statistics, and a chef I know stores all her recipes in a spreadsheet, including extremely specific quantities for spices and cook times for individual herbs. Who knew cooking could be so scientific? These days, spreadsheet applications are as common as e-mail and word processing. The structure they provide for storing information and performing calculations goes hand in hand with the increased readability of a well-designed spreadsheet.

The big name in spreadsheets these days is Microsoft Excel. The Excel application can be purchased individually for about $300, or you can get it as a bundle with the Microsoft Office suite of applications, starting at about $400. But as I mentioned in Chapter 5, Microsoft likes to update its Office products every three to four years; keeping up with the latest versions can get expensive fast.

But just like the OpenOffice word processor called Writer that I covered in Chapter 5, an OpenOffice equivalent to Microsoft Excel exists. It's called Calc, and it's 100 percent free with features galore.

This chapter is your introduction to this second of three OpenOffice applications (the third is OpenOffice Impress, covered in Chapter 7). I'll provide an overview of the application's interface and then show you some useful tasks you can perform.

Updating OpenOffice Calc

This chapter contains figures showing screen captures from OpenOffice Calc version 3.0. If you installed Ubuntu 8.10 (refer to Chapter 2), the OpenOffice applications are already installed with the operating system, but they are version 2.4, not the most recent version of the OpenOffice apps.

You can use OpenOffice version 2.4 if you like, but if you prefer to have the most recent version on your U-PC (and a much better and more stable version, in my opinion), please refer to the Chapter 5 section titled "OpenOffice Versions for Ubuntu" for instructions on updating your version of OpenOffice.

Welcome to Calc

To open OpenOffice Calc, click the Applications menu, select the Office group, and then click OpenOffice.org Spreadsheet, as shown in Figure 6-1.

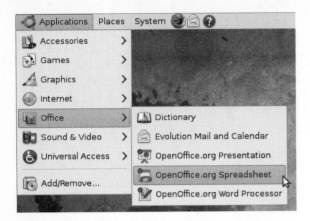

Figure 6-1. *Selecting OpenOffice.org Spreadsheet opens Calc.*

A new window opens (see Figure 6-2). This is the OpenOffice Calc 3.0 application.

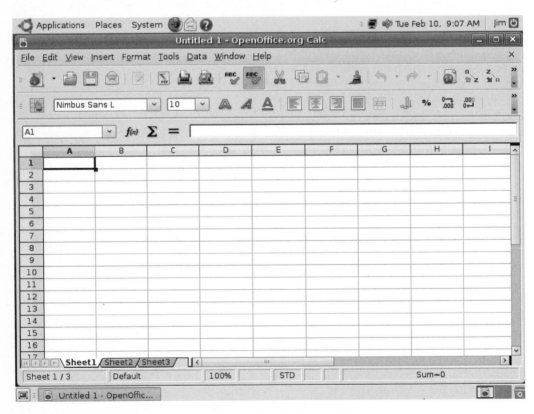

Figure 6-2. *OpenOffice Calc's user interface and a blank spreadsheet.*

Calc has a collection of drop-down menus that run along the top of the screen: File, Edit, View, Insert, Format, Tools, Data, Window, and Help. Below the menu bar are three additional toolbars. Figure 6-3 shows the first toolbar with descriptions of some of its buttons. Hover your mouse pointer over any button and you'll see a small tooltip window appear that describes that button's function. And on the extreme right edge of the first toolbar you'll see a small downward-pointing triangle that opens up additional features when clicked (also seen in Figure 6-3).

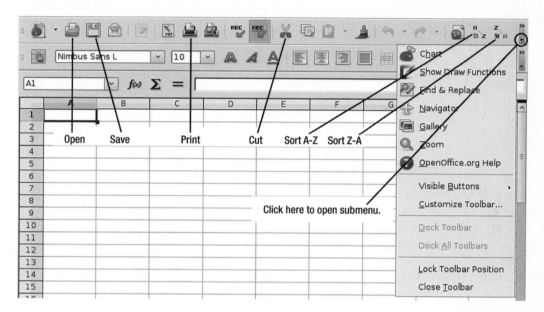

Figure 6-3. *The first toolbar includes buttons to print, save, sort, and more.*

Figure 6-4 shows Calc's second toolbar with some descriptions. Another menu of available tools can be accessed by clicking the downward-pointing arrow indicated in the figure.

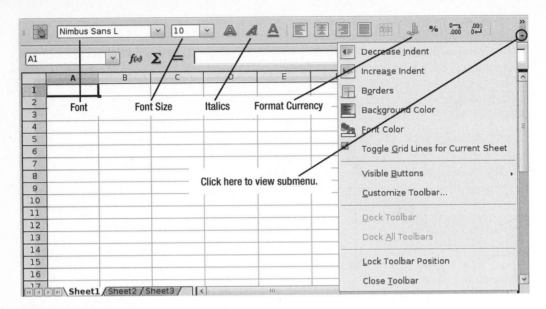

Figure 6-4. *Calc's second toolbar options for modifying the cells in a spreadsheet.*

Figure 6-5 shows Calc's third toolbar. The Cell Locator box always lets you know which cell or cells you have selected. Shortcuts to the Function Wizard as well as the Sum Function are also available. (I'll cover functions later in the chapter.) Finally, if you know how to use a certain function, you can type it directly into the Function Input Line without having to launch the Function Wizard—a real time-saver.

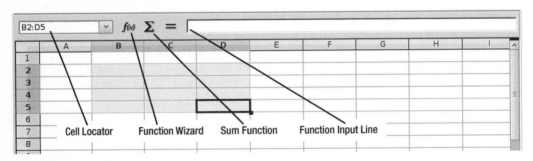

Figure 6-5. *The third toolbar is all about finding and using Calc's built-in functions.*

The bottom edge of Calc contains a fourth toolbar (see Figure 6-6). A nice feature on this toolbar is the Quick Sum feature; selected cells (such as the three cells shown in Figure 6-6 that contain 23, 42, and 39) are summed and the result displayed.

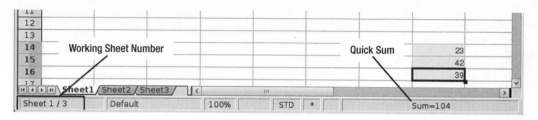

Figure 6-6. *Calc's bottom toolbar has a useful Quick Sum feature.*

You can also minimize, maximize, and close Calc by using the three buttons in the upper-right corner of the screen, as shown in Figure 6-7.

Figure 6-7. *Minimize, maximize, or close the Calc window.*

I'll be using these menus, buttons, and tools throughout the remainder of this chapter as I show you various tasks and features of Calc.

Using Calc

If you're new to spreadsheets, I recommend that you access the Help menu and select the OpenOffice.org Help option. When the OpenOffice.org Help window opens (see Figure 6-8), click Instructions for Using OpenOffice.org Writer and learn about the basics of using Calc. All the basic spreadsheet skills are covered here, including using the mouse pointer to select and enter data in a cell, selecting multiple cells, applying formatting to cells, renaming sheets, creating column headers, and more. The amount of help provided here is extensive, so be sure to check here first if you need more information about performing a task in Calc.

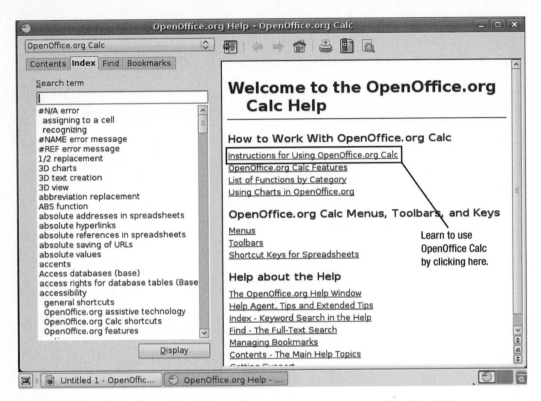

Figure 6-8. *OpenOffice.org Calc Help is the best source of information for using Calc.*

The following sections contain step-by-step instructions for performing some of the basic and advanced Calc tasks. Consult the Help Wizard shown in Figure 6-8 for additional details on any of these tasks.

Inserting a New Column between Existing Columns

Figure 6-9 shows a small collection of information stored under four columns (A, B, C, and D) with header names of First Name, City, Age, and High Score.

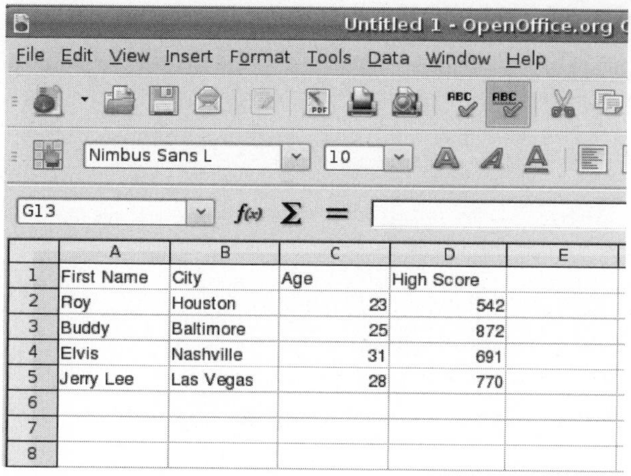

Figure 6-9. *Four columns of information in a simple spreadsheet.*

You could add a new header name (Last Name, for example) under the E column shown in Figure 6-9, but it would be more useful to place it between the A and B columns. To do this, click the letter B to select the B column. Next, click the Insert menu and choose the Columns option. Columns B, C, and D will be shifted to the right and a new column will be inserted, as shown in Figure 6-10. (Inserted columns always appear to the left of the selected column.)

Tip An easier way to add new columns is to simply right-click the top of a column (for example, column B in Figure 6-9) and then choose Insert Columns. Column B shifts to the right and is renamed as column C (see Figure 6-10). The new column is empty of data, of course.

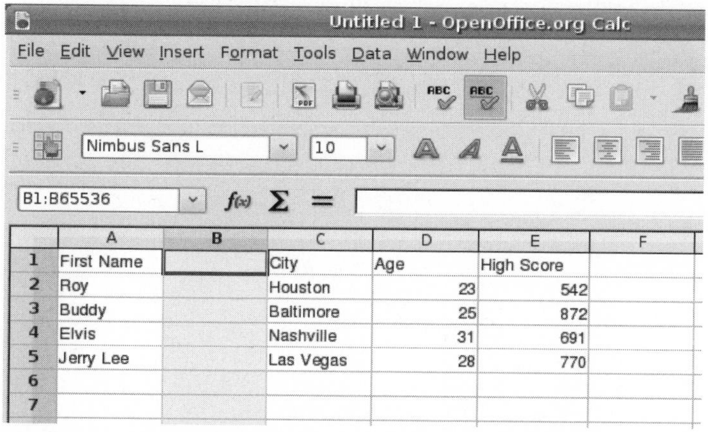

Figure 6-10. *A new column is inserted and will be labeled Last Name.*

Inserting a New Row Between Existing Rows

Figure 6-11 shows the updated collection of information stored under five columns—A, B, C, D, and—with header names of First Name, Last Name, City, Age, and High Score.

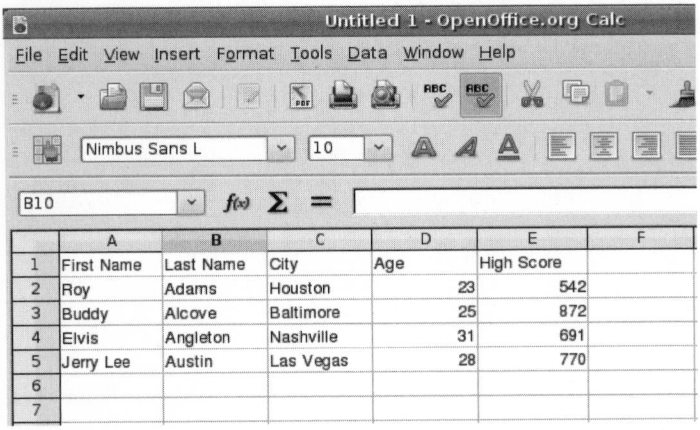

Figure 6-11. *A simple spreadsheet with five columns and four rows of data.*

Suppose that you want to insert a new row of information for Frankie Agathon. Notice that the current rows are listed alphabetically using the Last Name column (B). An inserted row is always added above a selected row, so in this example, you would click row 3 (Buddy Alcove) to select it. Next, click the Insert menu and choose the Rows option. The Buddy Alcove, Elvis Angleton, and Jerry Lee Austin information will be shifted down one row, as shown in Figure 6-12.

■**Tip** As with the previous tip on adding a new column, simply right-click the number of a row (for example, on row 2 in Figure 6-11) and choose Insert Rows. Row 2 shifts down and becomes row 3, as shown in Figure 6-12. The new row is empty and waiting for new data.

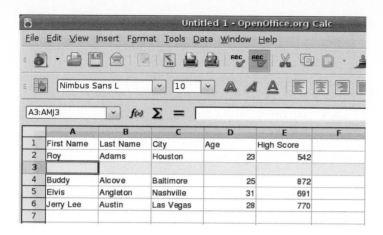

Figure 6-12. *A new row is inserted for Frankie Agathon's data.*

Sorting Information by Column

Figure 6-13 shows six rows of information for five individuals stored under five columns (the first row is used for the header titles).

	A	B	C	D	E	F
1	First Name	Last Name	City	Age	High Score	
2	Roy	Adams	Houston	23	542	
3	Frankie	Agathon	Caprica	28	1052	
4	Buddy	Alcove	Baltimore	25	872	
5	Elvis	Angleton	Nashville	31	691	
6	Jerry Lee	Austin	Las Vegas	28	770	
7						

Figure 6-13. *The user information is currently sorted alphabetically by last name.*

Columns typically contain text, numbers, or some alphanumeric combination (such as a street address that contains a number and text). Columns can be sorted depending on the information stored in their cells; for example, columns of numbers can be sorted highest-to-lowest or lowest-to-highest. Columns of text can be sorted alphabetically, A-to-Z or Z-to-A. Figure 6-13 shows that the list is currently sorted alphabetically using the Last Name column. To sort the data by a different column (High Score, in this example), select all the data that will be sorted, as shown in Figure 6-14. (Note that I did not select row 1, which contains the header names.)

	A	B	C	D	E	F
1	First Name	Last Name	City	Age	High Score	
2	Roy	Adams	Houston	23	542	
3	Frankie	Agathon	Caprica	28	1052	
4	Buddy	Alcove	Baltimore	25	872	
5	Elvis	Angleton	Nashville	31	691	
6	Jerry Lee	Austin	Las Vegas	28	770	
7						

Figure 6-14. *Select all the data that will be sorted and omit header names.*

Next, click the Data menu and select the Sort option. Figure 6-15 shows the Sort window that opens.

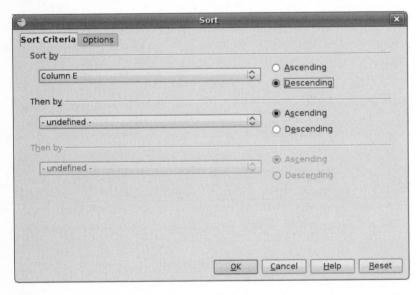

Figure 6-15. *The Sort window lets you select how your data will be sorted.*

As shown in Figure 6-15, click the first drop-down box, choose Column E, and select the Descending option. This process reorganizes the rows based on the High Score (column E), highest-to-lowest. Figure 6-16 shows the data sorted by High Score.

	A	B	C	D	E
1	First Name	Last Name	City	Age	High Score
2	Frankie	Agathon	Caprica	28	1052
3	Buddy	Alcove	Baltimore	25	872
4	Jerry Lee	Austin	Las Vegas	28	770
5	Elvis	Angleton	Nashville	31	691
6	Roy	Adams	Houston	23	542
7					

Figure 6-16. *All the rows are sorted based on column E.*

Using the Formula Wizard

Figure 6-17 shows an updated spreadsheet with two new columns: Completion Time (seconds) and Final Score. Although the High Score column is useful, the contest these five individuals competed in actually judges them based on time as well; scoring high in less time is the goal. To determine the winner, multiply the High Score value (in points) by the Completion Time value (in seconds) for each competitor and then sort the spreadsheet using the Final Score column to determine the final winner. The winner is the person with the highest Final Score.

	A	B	C	D	E	F	G
1	First Name	Last Name	City	Age	High Score	Completion Time (seconds)	Final Score
2	Frankie	Agathon	Caprica	28	1052	59	
3	Buddy	Alcove	Baltimore	25	872	38	
4	Jerry Lee	Austin	Las Vegas	28	770	52	
5	Elvis	Angleton	Nashville	31	691	43	
6	Roy	Adams	Houston	23	542	109	
7							

Figure 6-17. *The contest winner is the person with the highest Final Score.*

The first task is to calculate the Final Score. This is done by taking a competitor's High Score value and multiplying it by his Completion Time value. First, let's calculate the Final Score for Frankie Agathon (row 2). First, click Frankie's Final Score cell, G2, as shown in Figure 6-18.

■**Note** All cells in a spreadsheet use the letter/number naming convention. The letter designates the column, and the number designates the row. The column after Z starts with AA, then AB, and so on.

	A	B	C	D	E	F	G
1	First Name	Last Name	City	Age	High Score	Completion Time (seconds)	Final Score
2	Frankie	Agathon	Caprica	28	1052	59	
3	Buddy	Alcove	Baltimore	25	872	38	
4	Jerry Lee	Austin	Las Vegas	28	770	52	
5	Elvis	Angleton	Nashville	31	691	43	
6	Roy	Adams	Houston	23	542	109	
7							

Figure 6-18. *Frankie Agathon's Final Score is empty and needs to be calculated.*

Next, click the Formula Wizard button (refer to Figure 6-5); a window appears, similar to the one shown in Figure 6-19.

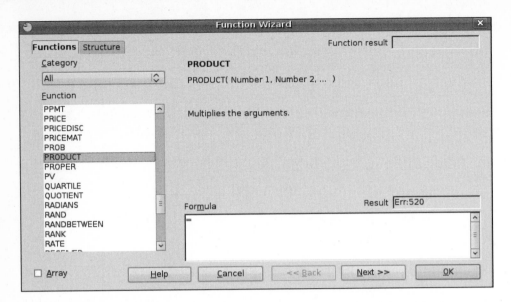

Figure 6-19. *The Function Wizard performs calculations using spreadsheet data.*

Scroll down the list of functions on the left side of the window and click PRODUCT, as shown in Figure 6-19, and click the Next button. Note that when you select a function, you can view a description of what that function does on the right side of the screen.

The window shown in Figure 6-20 appears, which is where you select the cells that will be used to calculate the Final Score. Notice the Number 1, Number 2, Number 3, etc. list. For each number, you can type in a cell name (such as E2) or click the small button indicated in the figure to hide this window until you click the desired cell.

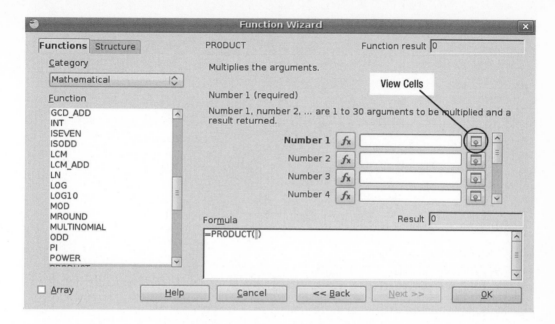

Figure 6-20. *You must select the cells that will be used by the function to generate a new result.*

I clicked that button for Number 1 and I selected cell E2 for Frankie's High Score (indi-cated by a blue box that surrounds the value). Press the Enter key to finalize the selection (see Figure 6-21).

	A	B	C	D	E	
1	First Name	Last Name	City	Age	High Score	Completic
2	Frankie	Agathon	Caprica	28	1052	
3	Buddy	Alcove	Baltimore	25	872	
4	Jerry Lee	Austin	Las Vegas	28	770	
5	Elvis	Angleton	Nashville	31	691	
6	Roy	Adams	Houston	23	542	
7						

Figure 6-21. *Select the first cell to be used in the calculation.*

After pressing Enter to accept the first value, Figure 6-22 shows that the cell E2 has been entered into the Number 1 field. I also performed the same steps described previously and selected cell F2 (Frankie's Completion Time) for the Number 2 field.

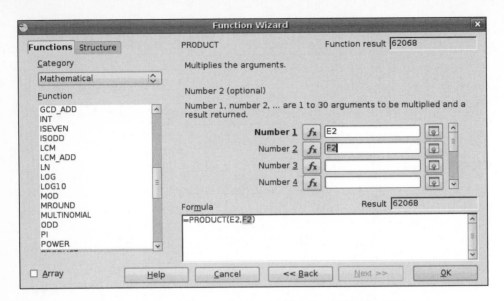

Figure 6-22. *Both cells used to calculate the Final Score have been selected.*

To calculate Frankie's Final Score, I click the OK button. Figure 6-23 shows the calculated value.

	A	B	C	D	E	F	G
1	First Name	Last Name	City	Age	High Score	Completion Time (seconds)	Final Score
2	Frankie	Agathon	Caprica	28	1052	59	62068
3	Buddy	Alcove	Baltimore	25	872	38	
4	Jerry Lee	Austin	Las Vegas	28	770	52	
5	Elvis	Angleton	Nashville	31	691	43	
6	Roy	Adams	Houston	23	542	109	
7							

Figure 6-23. *The Final Score value has been calculated.*

Figure 6-24 shows the same calculation performed for the remaining four rows.

	A	B	C	D	E	F	G
1	First Name	Last Name	City	Age	High Score	Completion Time (seconds)	Final Score
2	Frankie	Agathon	Caprica	28	1052	59	62068
3	Buddy	Alcove	Baltimore	25	872	38	33136
4	Jerry Lee	Austin	Las Vegas	28	770	52	40040
5	Elvis	Angleton	Nashville	31	691	43	29713
6	Roy	Adams	Houston	23	542	109	59078

Figure 6-24. *Calculate the Final Score for the remaining contestants.*

Figure 6-25 shows that the rows are sorted by the Final Score column, lowest to highest. Elvis wins!

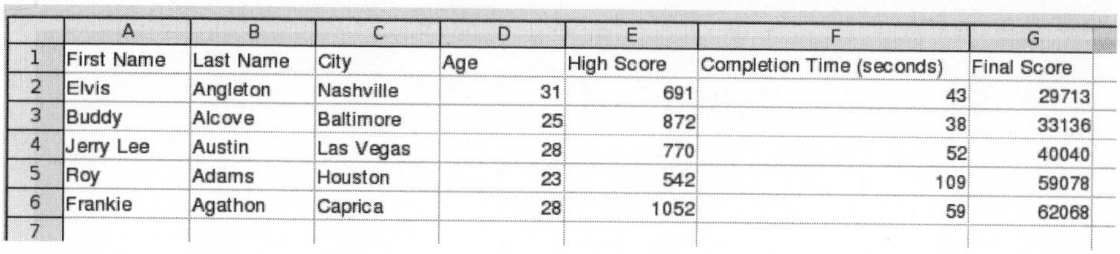

	A	B	C	D	E	F	G
1	First Name	Last Name	City	Age	High Score	Completion Time (seconds)	Final Score
2	Elvis	Angleton	Nashville	31	691	43	29713
3	Buddy	Alcove	Baltimore	25	872	38	33136
4	Jerry Lee	Austin	Las Vegas	28	770	52	40040
5	Roy	Adams	Houston	23	542	109	59078
6	Frankie	Agathon	Caprica	28	1052	59	62068
7							

Figure 6-25. *Sorting the list shows that Elvis is the King!*

Notice in Figure 6-26 that I selected a cell that contains a calculation performed using a function. The actual formula used to generate the calculation will be visible in the function toolbar; in this example, the formula is =PRODUCT(E2;F2); the two cells, E2 and F2, are the cells that are multiplied together to get the Final Score for Elvis. Over time, you'll probably learn the format of various formulas and save time by typing them directly into the formula bar instead of using the Function Wizard.

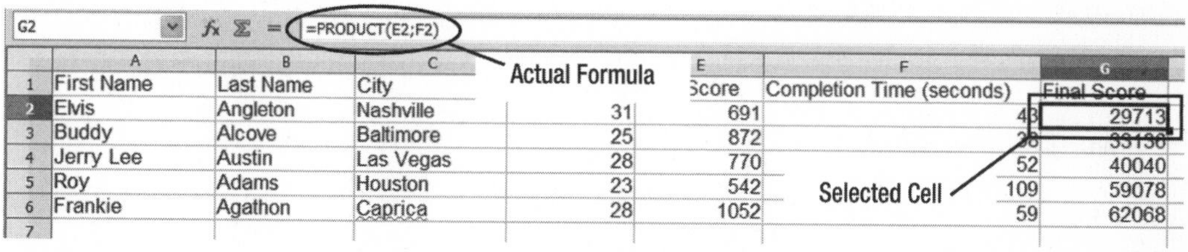

Figure 6-26. *The actual formula used to prove that Elvis is King!*

Summarizing Calc

Calc is my spreadsheet of choice. I used to be an Excel user, but the last time I purchased it was back in 2003 (Excel 2003, to be exact), and I really haven't found anything I needed Excel to do that I cannot do with Calc. Your mileage may vary, however. Calc is definitely full-featured, but there are many Excel power users out there who might have job requirements that Calc cannot fulfill. Your best bet is to open one of your existing spreadsheets in Calc and try it out—see whether all the functions, formatting, and other spreadsheet tools you need are supported in Calc. If you're like me, you'll find that your typical spreadsheet usage is limited to multiplying, dividing, sorting, and formatting cells.

As with OpenOffice Writer (refer to Chapter 5), remember that the official OpenOffice web forum found at http://user.services.openoffice.org/en/forum has a dedicated area just for Calc questions and is a great place to visit if you need help with Calc or any of its features. You'll find a supportive community of OpenOffice users ready to help you make the jump to Calc.

What's Next?

With OpenOffice Writer as your word processor and OpenOffice Calc as your spreadsheet application, let's round out your U-PC office suite by learning how to use OpenOffice Impress, a great slideshow application that works great by itself (or hand in hand with Calc and Writer) and lets you design some eye-catching presentations.

■■■

CHAPTER 7

Presentations with Impress

A few months back, I was asked to give a presentation in front of 200 people on the topic of Open Source software. The coordinator for the event called me and asked that I submit my PowerPoint presentation a few days early for review. I informed her that I could do that, but I wouldn't be using Microsoft PowerPoint. I could have heard a pin drop on the other end of the phone. I told her that it wouldn't make sense to create my slideshow on Open Source software on a non–Open Source application. She was a bit uncertain, but I told her to trust me; the presentation would be professional-looking and 100 percent compatible with her computer and with PowerPoint.

It's no surprise that when someone mentions the words *slideshow presentation*, PowerPoint comes to mind because it is generally considered to be the industry standard for slideshow design. But it's not the only game in town. Apple has its Keynote application for Mac users, for example. And when it comes to an open source software solution for creating slideshows, you'll be happy to hear that OpenOffice.org has its own player in the game. It's called Impress and (pardon the pun) it's impressive. Impress is 100 percent free, fully compatible with PowerPoint (it can save using the .ppt file extension), and it's easy to use—as you'll soon see.

This chapter will provide an overview of Impress's user interface and show you some features that are available when you're designing a slideshow. You'll be convinced that Impress is a viable solution to slideshow design and you'll save $300 or more by not having to purchase another product.

Updating OpenOffice Impress

This chapter contains figures showing screen captures from OpenOffice Impress version 3.0. If you installed Ubuntu 8.10, as described in Chapter 2, the OpenOffice applications are already installed with the operating system, but they are version 2.4, not the most recent version of the OpenOffice apps.

You can use OpenOffice version 2.4 if you like, but if you prefer to have the most recent version on your U-PC, please refer to the Chapter 5 section, "OpenOffice Versions for Ubuntu," for instructions on updating your version of OpenOffice.

Welcome to Impress

Open OpenOffice Impress by clicking the Applications menu and then selecting the Office group. Click OpenOffice.org Presentation, as shown in Figure 7-1.

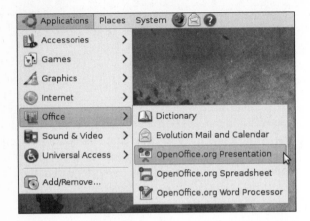

Figure 7-1. *Selecting OpenOffice.org Presentation opens Impress.*

The Impress 3.0 Presentation Wizard opens, as shown in Figure 7-2.

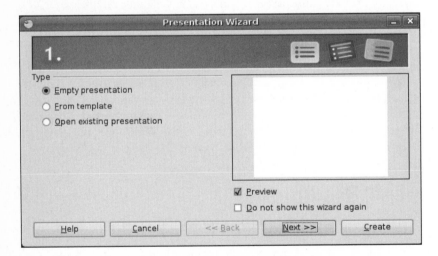

Figure 7-2. *The Impress Presentation Wizard offers you three choices.*

The Presentation Wizard allows you to choose from three options: opening an empty (new) presentation, opening a presentation template, or opening an existing presentation. For this example, I'll open an empty presentation; later in the chapter, I'll open a template and show you how that option works. Leave the "Empty presentation" default selection selected and click the Create button. The Impress application opens, as shown in Figure 7-3.

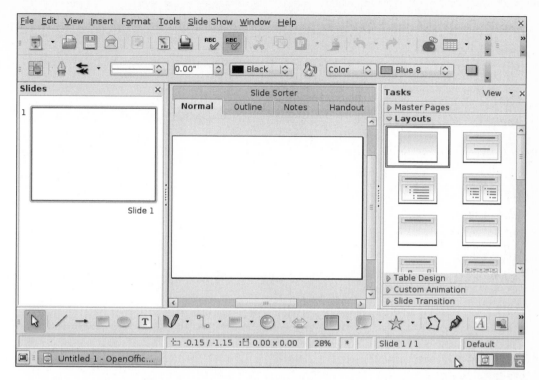

Figure 7-3. *A new Impress presentation file opens and is ready for your design.*

Figure 7-3 has a lot of options visible, but don't let the screen overwhelm you; many of the options can be hidden or will disappear after you begin designing your slideshow. You'll find a standard menu bar at the top that offers the following menus: File, Edit, View, Insert, Format, Tools, Slide Show, Window, and Help. Below the menu bar are two toolbars. Below the toolbars is the work area, and it's currently divided into three sections: Slides, Slide Sorter, and the Tasks window. At the very bottom of the screen are two more toolbars. Let me go over each of these toolbars briefly.

Figure 7-4 shows Impress's first toolbar with some descriptions. Two other drop-down menus containing additional tools can be accessed by clicking the downward-pointing arrows indicated in the figure.

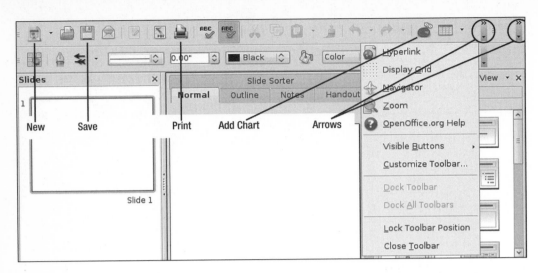

Figure 7-4. *Impress's first toolbar has many options, such as saving, printing, and zooming.*

Figure 7-5 shows Impress's second toolbar that offers formatting options for colors and text. A drop-down menu containing additional tools can be accessed by clicking the downward-pointing arrow indicated in the figure.

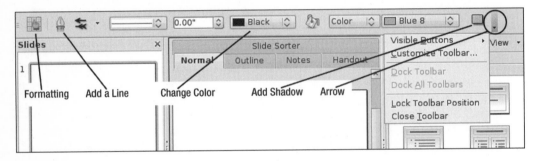

Figure 7-5. *Impress's second toolbar has formatting options that affect text, lines, and colors.*

Figure 7-6 shows Impress's three work area windows: Slides, Slide Sorter, and Tasks. As you add more slides to your presentation, you can view a thumbnail (small) version of a slide by clicking it in this list. The Slide Sorter window (in the middle) is where you actually modify a slide: add pictures, text, video, formatting, and more. Finally, the Tasks window offers a large collection of option screens; you can select a slideshow layout (shown in Figure 7-6) from the Layouts screen or add animation by clicking the arrow next on the Custom Animation screen (arrows for each screen are surrounded by squares in the figure). Additional screens include Master Pages, Table Design, and Slide Transition. I'll cover a few of these screens later in the chapter, but I recommend that you experiment with all of them and use the built-in Help feature to discover how they can be used to improve your slideshows.

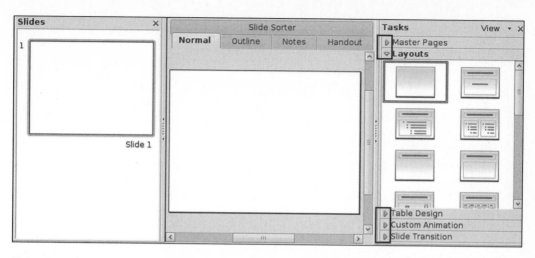

Figure 7-6. *Three work area windows are available for designing each slide.*

The Tasks window can be closed by clicking the x in the upper-right corner. You can close it to free up work area space and display a larger Slide Sorter window, as shown in Figure 7-7. To reopen the Tasks window, click the Format menu and choose Slide Layout. The Tasks window reappears in its original location.

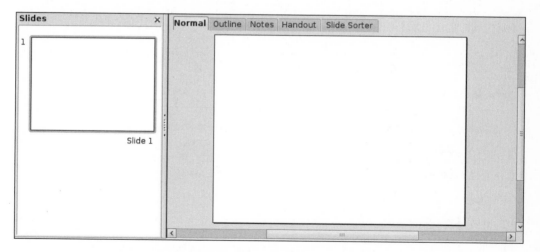

Figure 7-7. *Closing the Tasks window enlarges the Slide Sorter window.*

Figure 7-8 shows the third toolbar. A drop-down menu containing additional tools can be accessed by clicking the downward-pointing arrow indicated in the figure.

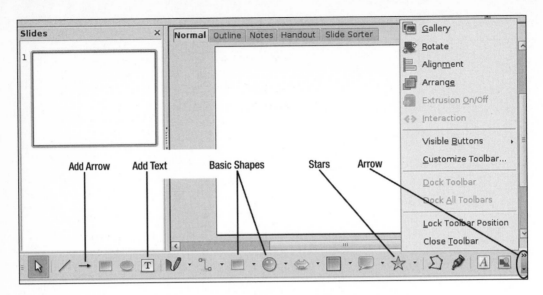

Figure 7-8. *Impress's third toolbar lets you add shapes, symbols, and more.*

The final bar at the very bottom (called the *status bar*) is shown in Figure 7-9. Among other things, this status bar provides the total number of slides you have in your presentation as well as the number for the slide you are currently viewing. In this example, I have a slideshow that consists of 5 slides and I'm viewing slide number 4 (4/5, or 4 of 5).

Figure 7-9. *Impress's status bar helps you remember which slide you are working on.*

As with the other OpenOffice applications, you can minimize, maximize, and close Impress by using the three buttons in the upper-right corner of the screen.

I'll be using all these menus, buttons, and windows throughout the remainder of this chapter as I show you the various tasks and features of Impress.

Using Impress

If you've never created a slideshow before, start by clicking the Help menu and then selecting the OpenOffice.org Help option. When the OpenOffice.org Help window opens (see Figure 7-10), click Instructions for Using OpenOffice.org Impress. Standard slideshow design skills are covered here, including adding new slides, choosing a template, importing video, and more. This should be your first stop when you have questions about performing tasks in Impress.

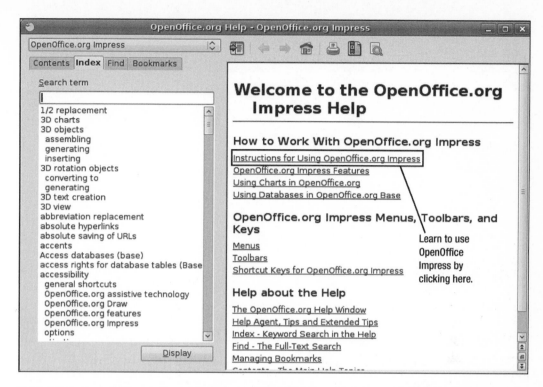

Figure 7-10. *OpenOffice.org Impress Help is the best source of information for using Impress.*

The following sections contain step-by-step instructions for performing some of the basic and advanced Impress tasks. Consult the Help Wizard shown in Figure 7-10 for additional details on any of these tasks.

Creating a Slideshow with a Theme

Figure 7-2 showed that you can create a blank slideshow or one with a theme. A blank slideshow is boring, quite frankly. So let's start over and create a new slideshow from scratch; click the File menu, select New, and then select Presentation. This time, select the "From template" option shown in Figure 7-11 and notice that a list of presentation themes is displayed near the bottom of the window. Scroll through that list until you find a color and style that you like and then click the Next button.

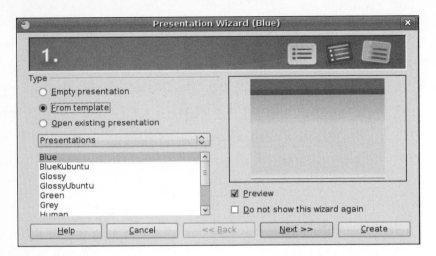

Figure 7-11. *Choose a template to give your slideshow some color and style.*

On the next screen (see Figure 7-12), you can choose to modify the background by selecting from the scrolling list that contains color changes, lines, and gradients. Feel free to experiment, but for this example I'll stay with my original theme and click the Next button.

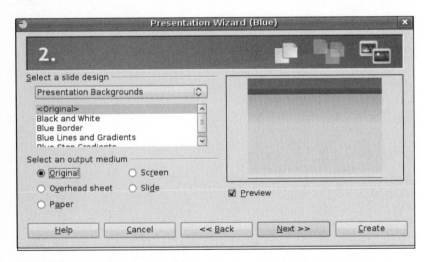

Figure 7-12. *You can modify the design with additional lines and colors.*

You can add transitions to your slideshows, such as making the current slide fade away or a new slide pushing on to the screen from the right or left. You can also control the speed of the transition. As seen in Figure 7-13, I selected to have my slides move from the right side of the screen to the left (Wipe Left) at a Fast speed. Experiment with the various effects and speeds to find something you like. Click the Next button when you finish.

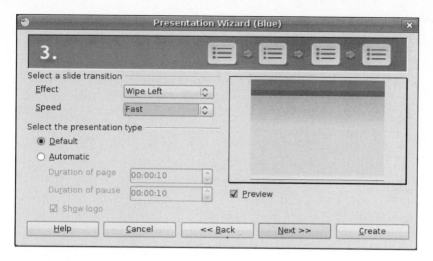

Figure 7-13. *Eye-catching transitions can be added to your slides.*

You can provide title information as well as a written summary about your slideshow on the next screen, as shown in Figure 7-14.

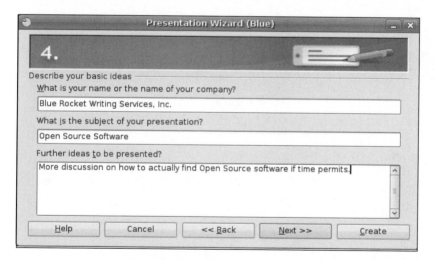

Figure 7-14. *Provide slideshow information such as company name and presentation subject.*

Click the Next button and you'll see a final screen, as shown in Figure 7-15. This gives you a summary of what your slides will look like in the preview window on the right. Use the Back button to make changes if you like or click the Create button to get started making your slideshow.

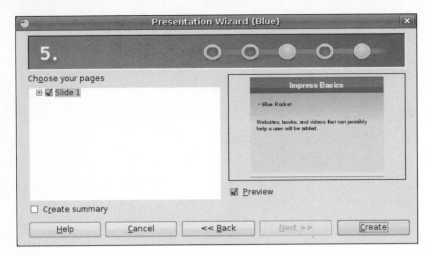

Figure 7-15. *The preview of your new slideshow is provided, or you can go back and make changes.*

Picking a Slide Layout

Figure 7-16 shows the screen after completing the Theme selection. On the right side of the screen under the Layouts bar, the slide's layout is indicated by the square border. Click any other layout to change the slide's design. Click the x in the upper-right corner of the Tasks window to close it and expand the Slide Sorter window.

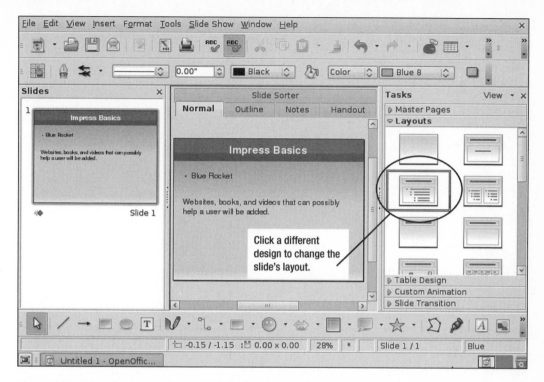

Figure 7-16. *Select from a variety of slide layouts using the Layouts bar.*

Figure 7-17 shows my first slide with a new layout. I can double-click the left side of the slide to add a photo or graphic stored on my hard drive as well as modify the text on the right side of the slide. I also closed down the Tasks window to give myself more room to work on the slide in the Slide Sorter window.

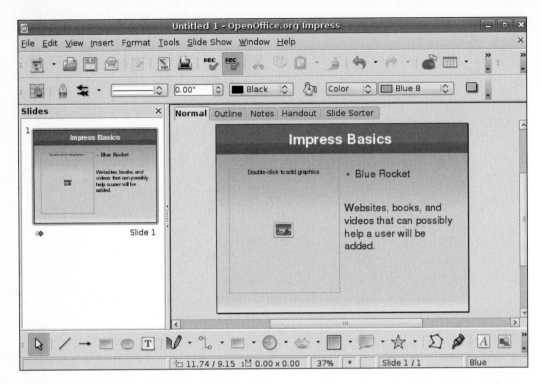

Figure 7-17. *Modify text and add pictures by editing the slide shown in the Slide Sorter window.*

Adding a New Slide

A slideshow with just one slide isn't a presentation. To add a new slide, click the Insert menu and click Slide. A new slide is always added after the slide that is currently selected; click a slide to select it, and an orange box surrounds it. Figure 7-18 shows a new slide added after the first one. Notice that the theme you selected is automatically applied to the new slide, and the Layouts pane reopens (if you closed it) so you can choose a layout.

■Tip An easier way to add a new slide is to simply right-click any empty space under the Slides column on the left side of the screen. Click the New Slide option that appears.

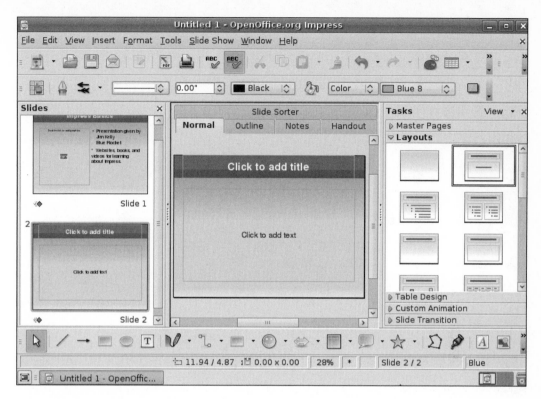

Figure 7-18. *A new slide retains the presentation theme you selected.*

Inserting a Video

Adding a video to be played inside a slide isn't difficult. Click the Insert menu and select the Movie and Sound option. Browse and locate the movie file on your hard drive and click the Open button. Your video is inserted into the slide, as shown in Figure 7-19. You can click and drag the movie and then place it by releasing the mouse button; resize the movie by clicking the video and using the small green squares surrounding the video.

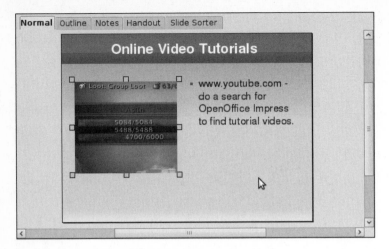

Figure 7-19. *Insert a video and resize it as desired.*

Creating Handouts

When giving a presentation, a speaker is often asked to provide handouts to the audience for note-taking or for easier viewing when the room is large. Click the File menu and select the Print option. The window shown in Figure 7-20 opens.

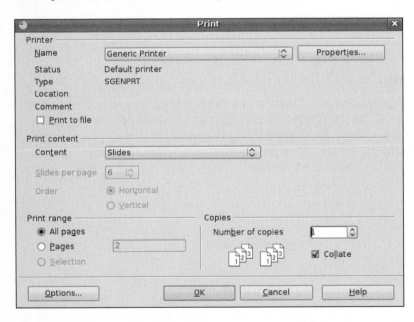

Figure 7-20. *There are numerous options for printing a slideshow.*

Click the drop-down menu labeled Content and choose Handouts, as shown in Figure 7-21. You can choose to display up to nine slides per page, horizontally or vertically.

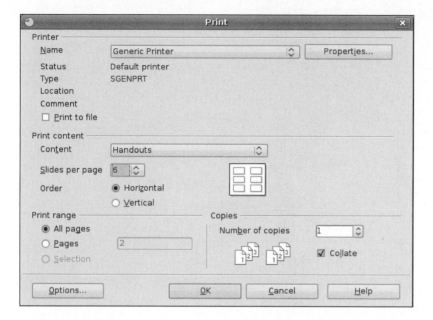

Figure 7-21. *Choose how many slides to print per page for the Handouts option.*

Rehearsing and Timing a Presentation

After completing a slideshow, many presenters often practice their presentation. Impress provides a built-in timer that can be used to help you determine whether you're spending too much time on a slide. Select the first slide in your presentation, click the Slide Show menu, and then select the Rehearse Timings option. Figure 7-22 shows a small timer in the lower-left corner of the screen. Practice your presentation and make note of the time it takes to complete the slide. When you click the Enter key or press the left mouse button, the next slide is loaded, and the timer resets.

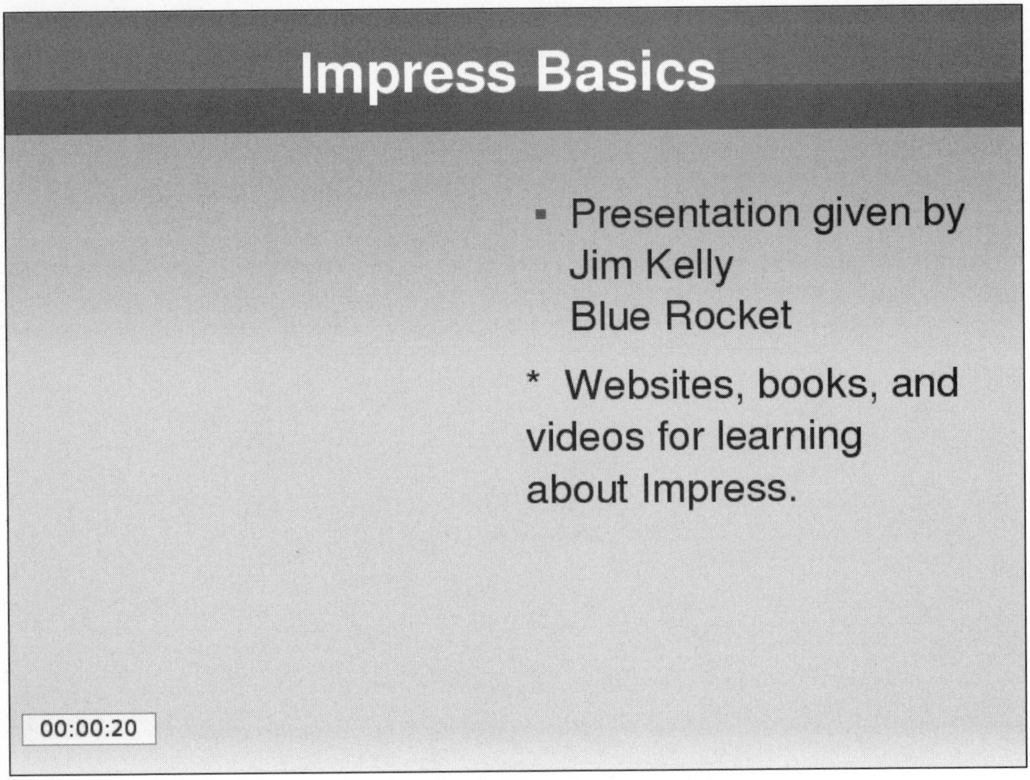

Figure 7-22. *The timer allows you to time and refine your speaking skills.*

Summarizing Impress

Back in Chapter 6, I told you that OpenOffice Calc was my spreadsheet of choice. For presentations, I switch back and forth between Impress and another slideshow app called Google Docs Presentation (which will be covered in Chapter 11). Impress definitely has a wealth of features and functions similar to Microsoft PowerPoint. I enjoy using it when I need to put together a quick presentation and I don't want to spend hours and hours tweaking every little setting. (I used to spend hours on a single slide in PowerPoint—not because I needed to, but because I could; sometimes having more features isn't the best solution.)

If you elect to use Impress as your slideshow application, I highly encourage you to visit http://www.openoffice.org and click the "I want to do more with my OpenOffice.org" link, as shown in Figure 7-23. The number of themes that comes preinstalled with Impress is small, but here you'll find a large collection of themes and clip art that can be downloaded for free and added to Impress (and other OpenOffice.org apps). Be sure to check out the SimpleTemplate One add-on for an interesting and eye-catching new theme. (You can also get it directly by visiting http://extensions.services.openoffice.org/project/simpletemplateone.)

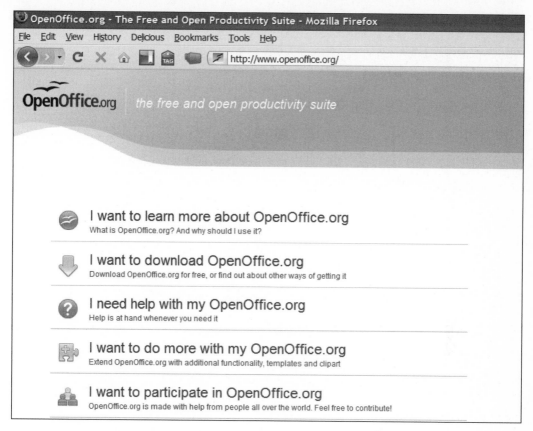

Figure 7-23. *OpenOffice.org provides additional themes and content for all OpenOffice apps.*

What's Next?

Impress rounds out the three OpenOffice applications covered in this book (refer to Chapter 5 and Chapter 6 for Writer and Calc, respectively). But you'll want (and need) more than just a word processor, spreadsheet, and slideshow application for your U-PC.

In Chapter 8, I'll show you one of the most powerful and popular photo editing applications available: Picasa. This application is not only 100 percent free but it's also already installed thanks to the Ubuntu operating system you installed on your PC. Get ready to learn some fun (and powerful) photo editing skills.

■■■

Photo Management with Picasa

The holiday season ended about a month ago as I write this, and I brought home hundreds of digital photos of family and friends. Most of these photos were taken indoors, so some of them have all kinds of lighting problems (I refuse to acknowledge that for many of them I forgot to turn on the flash). I also have a really cute photo of my nieces and nephews playing together, but unfortunately all of them have glowing red eyes, seriously reducing the cuteness factor. My camera has a red-eye reduction setting, but it's a pain to turn on and off, and it really drains the battery.

Fortunately for me, I have a secret weapon on my U-PC that lets me fix all these problems, and it's from a company you might have heard of in the news: Google. Yes, Google has a free application called Picasa that works great with the Ubuntu operating system. Picasa can fix red-eye, crop photos, solve lighting issues, and much more. Once you start using it, you'll stop fretting over red-eye and other problems with your digital pictures.

Picasa is so simple to use that I worry this chapter might actually slow you down; it's entirely possible for you to begin using Picasa and learn as you go—it's that easy to figure out. But I still want to provide an overview of Picasa as well as some examples of tasks you'll likely perform often on your photos. So let me show you why you don't need to spend $100 or even $25 on any photo-editing software; Picasa is here to rescue your digital pictures.

Getting Picasa

Picasa does not come preinstalled with the Ubuntu operating system. You'll need to go and download the installation file. Trust me; this is one of the easiest applications to download and install. How easy? Three steps:

1. Open the Firefox web browser and visit `http://www.picasa.com`. Click the Download Picasa 3 for Linux (beta) button, as shown in Figure 8-1.

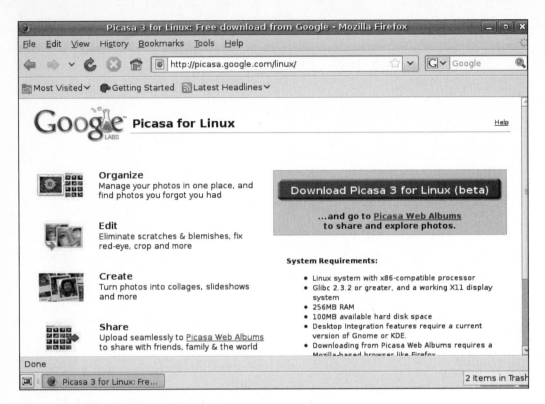

Figure 8-1. *Picasa can be downloaded from Google for free.*

2. Click the "deb, for Debian/Ubuntu i386" link and download the installation file, as indicated in Figure 8-2. If you have a 64-bit processor, click the (64-bit) option below it. (By default, the file will download to your Ubuntu desktop.)

■**Note** As I write this chapter, Picasa version 3 is still in beta; this might have changed by the time you read this. Version 2.7 does not run well on Ubuntu 8.10, the version of Ubuntu used in this book.

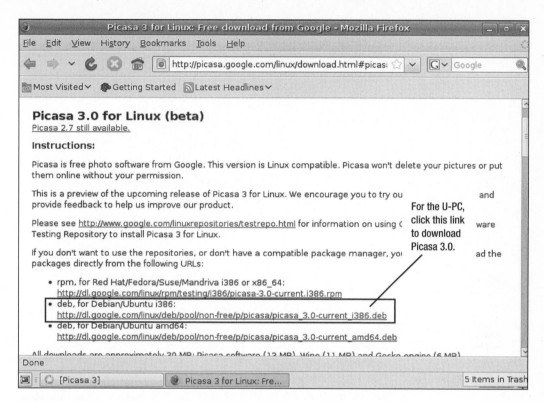

Figure 8-2. *Download the .deb file that will let you install Picasa on Ubuntu.*

3. Locate the Picasa installation file that was downloaded and double-click it. A Package Installer window will open; click the Install Package button in the upper-right corner, and the application installation will begin. You might be asked to provide an administrative password. If so, provide the password and click OK. When the installation is done, you can delete the installation file.

Welcome to Picasa

Open Picasa by clicking the Applications menu, selecting the Graphics group and then the Picasa listing. Click Picasa in the fly-out menu, as shown in Figure 8-3.

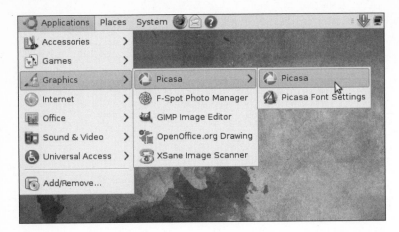

Figure 8-3. *The Picasa application can be found in the Graphics application category.*

WHAT ABOUT GIMP?

You might have noticed that installing Ubuntu also installs an application called GIMP Image Editor in the Graphics group (refer to Figure 8-3). Why would you want to download, install, and use Picasa instead of the built-in GIMP? Well, one of the main reasons why I recommend Picasa is its simplicity (and the fact that it's free). GIMP is an amazing application, and all the things you can do with Picasa (cropping, removing red-eye, and more) can be done with GIMP, but not as easily (in my opinion).

Entire books have been written on using GIMP. (For me, Apress publishes the best book on the subject: *Beginning GIMP, 2nd Edition*, by Akkana Peck.) It's one of the most powerful image editing applications available and it's 100 percent free. Feel free to open it up and play around. But I feel a quick warning is required here: GIMP can be a little overwhelming at first glance, but it's not a difficult application to learn, so I highly recommend that you purchase a book or consult some of the online resources such as the GIMP Online Manual (http://docs.gimp.org/en/) or some of the online tutorials (http://www.gimp.org/tutorials/) to get the most out of the application.

The first time you open Picasa, you need to read through the license agreement and click the Next button (see Figure 8-4) to see another page of the agreement. Click the I Agree button to continue.

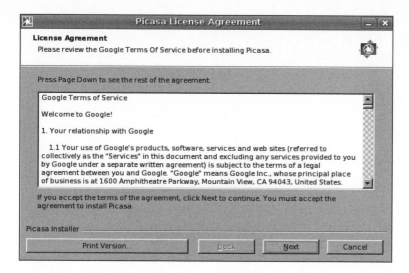

Figure 8-4. *As with most software, Picasa has a license agreement for you to read.*

The first time you install Picasa, it scans the entire hard drive for images, which can take some time, especially if you have thousands of digital photos stored on your computer. When the scan is done, you'll see a screen like the one shown in Figure 8-5.

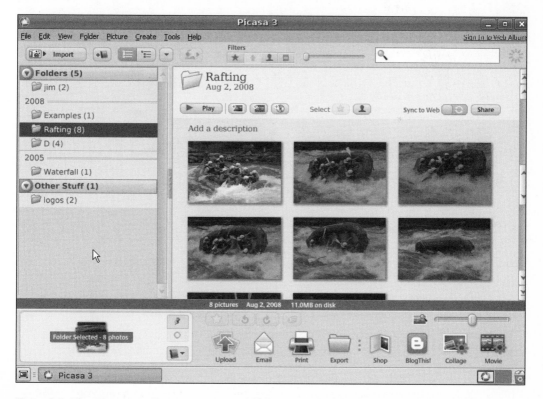

Figure 8-5. *The Picasa application opens with folders on the left and photos on the right.*

Tip I highly encourage you to begin a habit of storing your photos in the Photos folder on Ubuntu because you'll likely always find what you're looking for in there (it's so easy to remember). To access this folder, click the Places menu and select Photos. You can create as many subfolders in the Photos folder as you like. I'll show you later in the chapter how to configure Picasa to scan only the Photos folder and prevent Picasa from scanning the entire hard drive.

In Figure 8-5, you can see a folder structure running down the left side of the application. These are folders that Picasa has found on your computer that contain one or more images. If you click a photo, the images in that folder are displayed on the right under the Photo section. Folders are organized by year, newest to oldest. (If you look closely at the figure, you can see I have a photo from 2005.) Some cameras mark the digital files with dates, and Picasa can read this information to further help you organize your photos.

To see a larger view of a photo and to access tools to edit that photo, double-click the photo; it opens as shown in Figure 8-6. (Later in the chapter, I'll be showing you how to use some of the editing tools available.)

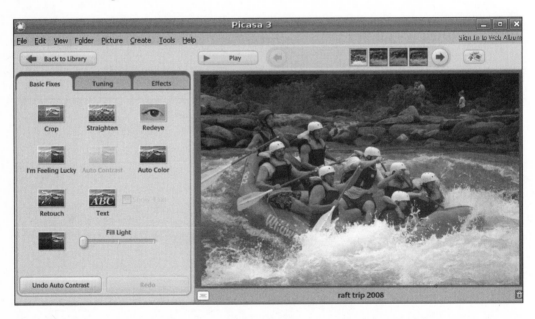

Figure 8-6. *Opening a photo provides access to editing tools on the left side of the screen.*

As you edit photos (for example, remove red-eye or crop a picture to remove unwanted parts of a photo), the changes are shown onscreen. You can always undo a change by clicking the Undo button; Figure 8-6 shows that I can undo an Auto-Contrast modification I made to this photo. (If you click Undo and change your mind again, click the Redo button; whatever modification you made will be added back to the photo.)

The final area of Picasa runs along the bottom of the application (see Figure 8-7). This toolbar allows you to do many things with your photos, including printing, sending photos via e-mail, uploading photos to the Internet, and even purchasing prints online. I'll go over a few of these features later in the chapter, but feel free to click and experiment—you really can't do anything to your pictures that can't be undone.

Figure 8-7. *Picasa's toolbar has numerous options, including printing and e-mailing photos.*

Before you move on to some sample Picasa tasks, I suggest that you make one change to the way Picasa scans your hard drive for images. Click the Tools menu and select the Folder Manager option. The Folder Manager window opens (see Figure 8-8).

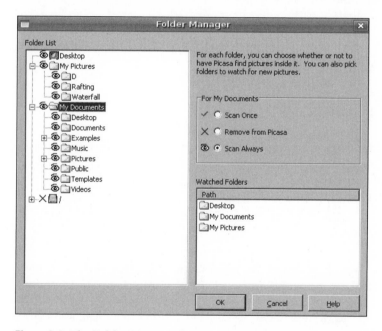

Figure 8-8. *The Folder Manager lets you decide what folders get scanned by Picasa.*

As shown in Figure 8-8, I expanded the My Pictures folder and the My Documents folder by clicking the + symbols next to them. I can now view all the subfolders. The little eye symbol shows that this folder is scanned by Picasa every time I run the application. There's really no need for Picasa to look under some of these folders—the Music, Videos, and Templates folders are not likely to hold my digital photos.

Click a folder that you want to remove from Picasa's scan and click the Remove from Picasa radio button, as indicated in Figure 8-9. Do this for each folder you want to have Picasa ignore on later startups. In this example, I selected the Music folder (among others) and clicked the Remove from Picasa option (notice that the eye symbol has changed to a red x). This indicates that the Music folder will not be searched in the future.

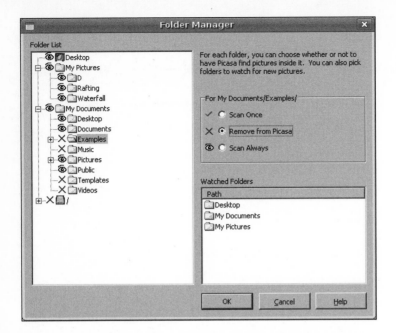

Figure 8-9. *Picasa no longer searches for images in folders shown with an x.*

When you finish, click the OK button. The next time you open Picasa, those folders you deselected will no longer be searched.

And now let's take a look at some useful Picasa features that you're sure to find useful when managing your digital photo collection.

Using Picasa

As you begin using Picasa, be aware that the application has a great built-in Help feature that can be accessed by clicking the Help menu and choosing the Help Contents and Index option. The Help web site shown in Figure 8-10 opens. Enter your question in the Search bar at the top and click the Search Picasa Help button to find articles and tutorials that might assist you.

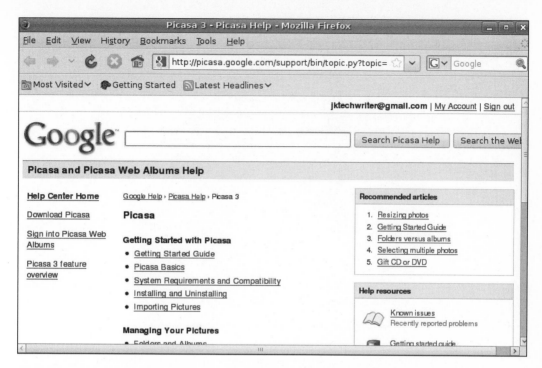

Figure 8-10. *The Picasa Help web site is a great place to look for answers and how-tos.*

Additional help with Picasa can be found by clicking the Help menu and choosing the Picasa Forums option. You can also visit `http://groups.google.com/groups/ Google-Labs-Picasa-for-Linux` and either post your question there or search for existing answers from previous posts.

Removing Red-eye

Nothing ruins a picture faster than a pair of glowing red eyes staring back at you. Many digital cameras can automatically remove red-eye, but it typically requires turning on a feature that gives a preflash followed by the actual flash of the camera. This can drain batteries, and the feature is typically not needed for outdoor photographs. But don't worry about red-eye anymore! Picasa has made removing red-eye extremely simple. Here's how it's done.

First, locate the photo with red-eye in the folder listing along the left side of Picasa. Double-click the photo to open it. As shown in Figure 8-11, click the Redeye button on the Basic Fixes tab (take note of the other two tabs—Tuning and Effects—that I'll cover shortly).

Figure 8-11. *Select the Redeye button to remove red-eye from a photo.*

Hold down the mouse button and drag a small box around one of the subject's eyes, as shown in Figure 8-12. Try to make the box as small as possible so it surrounds only the red portion of the eye. Release the mouse button, and the red-eye is removed. Perform the same action on the other eye. If you find that you need to zoom in on the photo for accuracy, drag the Zoom toolbar (indicated in Figure 8-12) to the right to zoom in and to the left to zoom back out. When you zoom in on a photo, a small version of the complete photo appears in the lower-right corner of the enlarged image. Drag the small white box with the mouse until it contains the area you want to work on; this works for red-eye as well as other editing tools such as cropping.

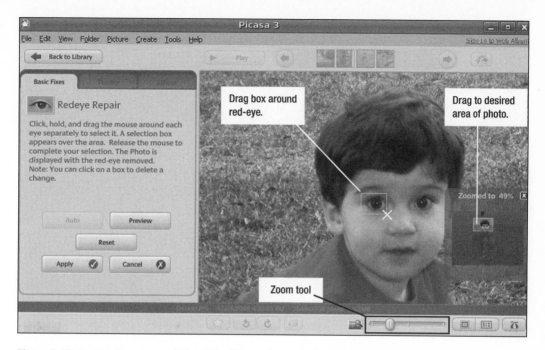

Figure 8-12. *Drag a box around the offending red-eye and it's gone in moments.*

Cropping a Photo

I took the photo of my son quickly and couldn't center the subject perfectly and keep his cousin's legs (just above his head) out of the picture (see Figure 8-13). But Picasa lets me easily edit this photo and crop the legs out of the photo using the Crop button indicated in the figure.

Figure 8-13. *Use the crop button to remove unwanted legs from an otherwise nice photo.*

The Crop Photo window shown in Figure 8-14 offers you three preconfigured crops to choose from. You can also click the drop-down list and select to either manually select the area of a photo to keep or select a preset size (such as 4×6 inches or 5×7).

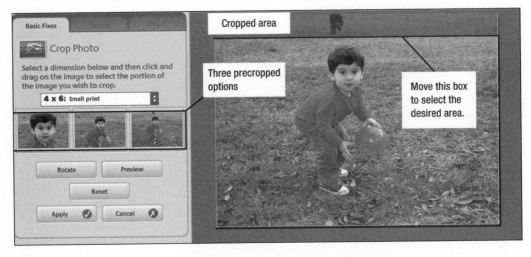

Figure 8-14. *Select a precropped image or make your own area selection.*

I select the 4×6 option; a box appears on the screen, and I can drag that area around as needed—up, down, left, and right—until I'm happy with the selection. I click the Apply button, and the photo is cropped as shown in Figure 8-15.

Figure 8-15. *No more legs in the picture!*

Adding Tags for Faster Searching

If you have hundreds or even thousands of digital photos stored on your hard drive, it can take quite some time to locate a specific photo. Even if you've titled your photos (such as *birthday154.jpg*), you still have to open them to see exactly who or what they display, or scan through thumbnails of all your photos looking (squinting, actually) for that one specific photo. It's a hassle, but Picasa offers a much better method.

Look back at Figure 8-15 and look under the photo for the text "Make a caption!" Click that line once and enter a description or keywords that reflect who or what is in the photo; press the Enter key when you finish. Figure 8-16 shows that I provided numerous keywords (or tags) for this photo.

Figure 8-16. *Add a caption to a photo using as many descriptives as possible.*

Notice that I included the month and year, the location (Florida), and, in this case, an age (21 months). Let's say I have a few thousand photos on my hard drive and I'm looking for all the photos that were taken in Florida. With Picasa, all I need to do is type the word *florida* on the search bar, as shown in Figure 8-17, and any photos that contain that tag (keyword) show up. You can enter multiple tags separated by a space or comma, and Picasa shows all photos with tags that match one or more of the tags.

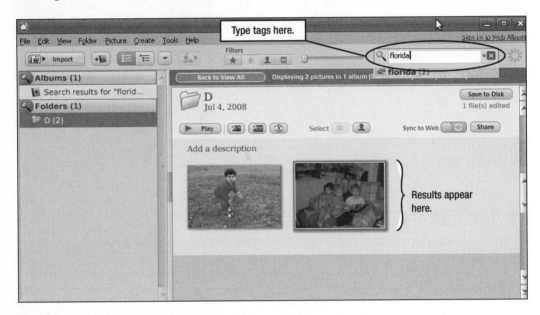

Figure 8-17. *Search using keywords, and matching photos will appear.*

Fixing Lighting Problems

Take a look at Figure 8-18; it might be difficult for you to see it, but the photo is just a little too dark. You have quite a few options on the left side of the screen; the Auto Contrast, Auto Color, and even I'm Feeling Lucky buttons all can work miracles. These buttons are found on the Basic Fixes tab.

Figure 8-18. *The Basic Fixes tab offers you options for editing a photo.*

For this photo, however, I want to work from the Tuning tab to manually control some of the settings such as color, shadow, and temperature using the drag bars indicated in Figure 8-19.

Figure 8-19. *The Tuning tab gives you more control over lighting settings.*

The final results are shown in Figure 8-20. Not too bad! Notice that I didn't need to use the Highlights or Shadows sliders. The water looks just like it did the day of the rafting trip, and the colors are much more vivid.

Figure 8-20. *Tuning changes can vastly improve the quality of a digital photo.*

Purchasing Photos Online

One of the nicest features of Picasa is how easily the application makes purchasing prints of your photos. You first create a virtual album by selecting a photo that you want to purchase and then click the green pin button, as indicated in Figure 8-21. The pin keeps the selected photos in the Album section until you're done picking all the photos you want to order. (Click the red circle below the green pin to deselect all photos.)

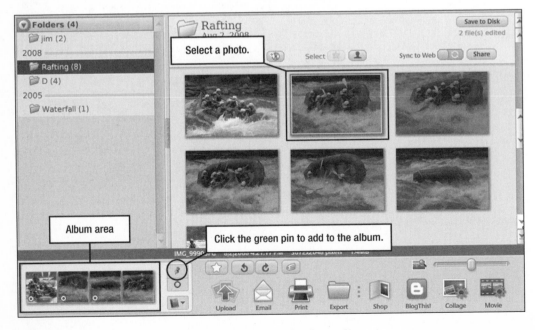

Figure 8-21. *Pin photos to keep in the album for purchasing online.*

After you select all the photos you want to purchase, click the Shop button on the Picasa toolbar. A window opens (see Figure 8-22). You'll see a listing of companies that offer to print your photos for you at a price much lower than you'll find at a local photo kiosk or developer. Click the Choose button for a few (or all) of the companies and compare their prices; pick the one that works best for you and follow the onscreen instructions for submitting your photos via Picasa. The photos will be printed, boxed, and shipped to you. How easy is that?

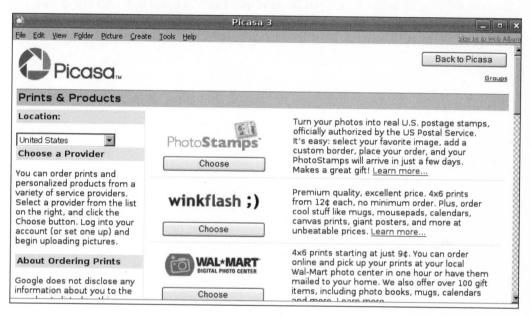

Figure 8-22. *Picasa offers links to a variety of photo printing services; shop for the best price.*

Summarizing Picasa

I've been able to show you only a handful of Picasa's features, but I hope you got a glimpse of how easy Picasa is to use. You really can't make a mistake with this application; all the editing features can be reversed by clicking the Undo button, and the Picasa toolbar offers additional services such as the ability to upload your photos to a blog, e-mail them to friends and family, and even upload them to the Picasa Web Albums service that stores photos online.

Remember that Picasa has both an online forum and online Help documentation that you can access to learn about every little feature this application has to offer. Get familiar with all its features, and you'll find that managing and editing your digital photos is no longer a chore.

What's Next?

Chapter 9 is all about web browsing, but not with just any web browser. When it comes to accessing web pages, there are dozens of different web browsers out there that can do the job. But would you be interested in using a web browser that can be modified with add-ons that provide extra functions and powers, far beyond the abilities of the common web browser? Then keep reading, because up next you'll learn how to super-charge your web browsing.

CHAPTER 9

Web Browsing with Firefox

The Internet has changed the world. Going online, you can buy books, research a potential vehicle purchase, check for movie times (and even buy and print tickets), download software, view videos, and find 1,001 ways to distract yourself. And all these activities have two things in common: they require a web browser and a connection to the Internet.

Most operating systems these days come prepackaged with a web browser. Microsoft, for example, provides Internet Explorer (IE) with all its Windows operating system installations, and Apple provides Safari with the Mac OS.

For your U-PC running the Ubuntu operating system, you'll find a prepackaged web browser called Firefox; some of you might already be familiar with it because it runs on Windows and Macs, too. Firefox by itself is fairly easy to use: open the browser, type in a web address, and you're surfing the Web. But Firefox is more than just a web browser as you'll soon learn. In this chapter, I'll cover the basics of using Firefox as well as show you how to personalize the browser and make it more useful to you.

Welcome to Firefox

Firefox is preinstalled with the Ubuntu operating system. There's nothing to download to get the basic browser, and Ubuntu doesn't even make you click any menus to launch it. To open Firefox, simply click the icon indicated in Figure 9-1.

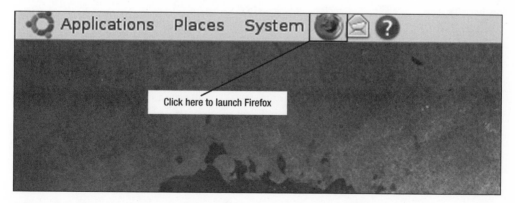

Figure 9-1. *Firefox comes preinstalled and can be launched using this little icon.*

The Firefox application opens, as shown in Figure 9-2.

Figure 9-2. *Firefox opens to the Ubuntu start page with a Google search box.*

■Note The version of Firefox installed during my Ubuntu installation is 3.0.5. Your version might differ, but the functionality should be similar to the steps described in this chapter.

The Firefox window has a few different areas that I want to cover before you move into some more advanced uses of the browser. You'll notice a familiar strip of menus running along the very top of the Firefox browser (refer to Figure 9-2). The list of menus includes File, Edit, View, History, Bookmarks, Tools, and Help. You'll visit some of these menus later in the chapter, but feel free to click and experiment to see what's available.

Just below the menus is the toolbar shown in Figure 9-3. You'll be using this toolbar frequently, so let me explain each button quickly.

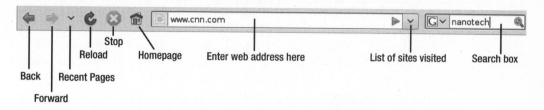

Figure 9-3. *The Firefox toolbar holds only the most necessary buttons and fields for browsing.*

As you visit more and more web sites and pages, you can use the Back button to return to previous pages; one click reloads the previous web page you viewed, two clicks reload the page before that one, and so on. The Forward button does the reverse; click it to jump ahead after you use the Back button a few times.

The Reload button is useful for refreshing the current screen without changing the page. For pages that provide information that changes frequently (such as financial web sites that display a constant stock price or a weather web site that updates the temperature every few minutes), clicking the Reload page forces the web browser to refresh whatever data is available for that page. The Stop button, likewise, can stop a Reload or stop a new web page from loading if you click it fast enough. (Most web pages load so quickly that you won't have time to click the Stop button if you change your mind.)

Every time you open your web browser, it displays your homepage. Figure 9-2 shows that the Ubuntu start page is the default homepage when you first open Firefox, but you can change your homepage to any web site you like; I'll show you how to do this shortly. Whenever you're browsing the Internet, a click of the Homepage button takes you immediately to your preset homepage.

Enter web addresses in the web address field indicated in Figure 9-3. Enter addresses in the form of http://www.website.com or simply website.com (Firefox is smart enough to add the http://www part). You can click the downward-pointing arrow to the right of the address field to see a list of recently viewed web addresses you've visited.

Finally, Firefox offers a Search box at the far right of the toolbar; type in your text to search and click the small magnifying glass button, and your search results will be displayed in the browser window below the toolbar.

Below the Firefox toolbar is the Bookmarks toolbar shown in Figure 9-4.

Figure 9-4. *Additional information can be found on the Bookmarks toolbar.*

If you're new to Firefox or to web browsing in general, clicking the Getting Started button takes you to an online tutorial with more help than you can imagine. Feel free to take a few tours—the button remains there in case you ever have a question. When you feel you've gotten all you can get from the button, simply right-click it and choose Delete. The Getting Started button will be removed.

The Most Visited drop-down list is helpful; click this button and you can see a list of the ten web sites you visit most often. Below the list is the option to Open All in Tabs, which does exactly that: all ten web sites open in their own tabs, displayed below the secondary toolbar.

Click the Latest Headlines button, and a list of all the latest news stories appear. Select a news item and it opens in the browser window.

This Bookmarks toolbar can hold many different buttons, and I'll show you how to customize it a bit later in the chapter.

Using Firefox

Firefox functions like every other web browser when it comes to giving you access to a web address. You simply type in the web address, press Enter, and the destination web site appears on your screen. Web browsers are definitely useful and reliable, but they're also fairly boring. The basic features I described previously (such as the Back button, the Search field, and the Homepage button) are fairly typical of all web browsers.

Given these basic features, there's not much difference in your choice of browser. Fortunately for you, however, not all web browsers are created equal, and Firefox is one browser that rises above the rest because it offers something called the add-on. And add-ons (100 percent free) are where Firefox truly shines. There is simply no way to accurately describe an add-on because there are so many variations. Think of an add-on as an upgrade to the Firefox browser, with add-ons functioning as miniapplications embedded within Firefox. What add-ons are available—I'm glad you asked.

Finding Add-ons

To get a better idea of what an add-on is and what it does, let's take a look at what's currently available. Click the Tools menu and select the Add-ons option, as shown in Figure 9-5.

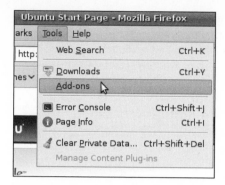

Figure 9-5. *Finding add-ons starts under the Tools menu.*

The Add-ons window appears (see Figure 9-6).

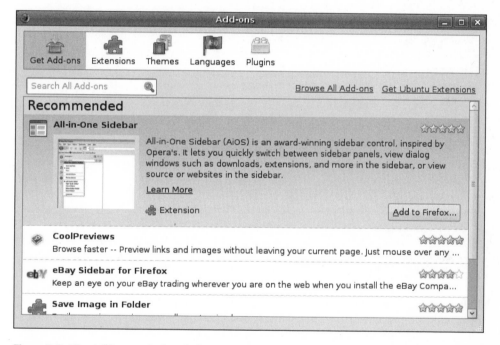

Figure 9-6. *The Add-ons window helps you narrow your search for add-ons.*

The Add-ons window gives you a listing of recommended add-ons along with a brief description of what each add-on does. Each add-on is rated with between one and five stars by users, so you can use this as a possible gauge of what is useful and what isn't. Feel free to scroll down the list and see what's recommended; when done, click the Browse All Add-ons link in the upper-right corner of the window. Figure 9-7 shows the Firefox Add-ons tab that appears.

Figure 9-7. *Search for Firefox Add-ons that can make your browser even more useful.*

Right now, you probably aren't aware of which add-ons are available, so the search text box in the middle of the screen isn't that useful. As you become more familiar with add-ons, you can start searching for them by typing in the name or a brief description of what you want

Firefox to be able to do. But for now, let's go hunting for a specific add-on using the categories listed down the left side of the screen. Click the Bookmarks category; the window shown in Figure 9-8 appears. Click the Most Popular First link on the right side of the page.

Figure 9-8. *Locate the add-on you want to learn about and click its download link.*

I scrolled down the list of various bookmark add-ons that appears and located Delicious Bookmarks (one of my favorite add-ons), as shown in Figure 9-9.

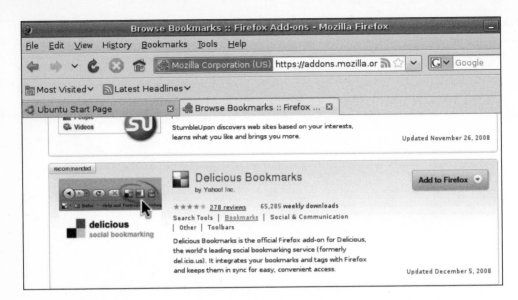

Figure 9-9. *An information screen provides reviews, details, and a button to add to Firefox.*

You can click the add-on name to read a more detailed description of what service the add-on provides; if you want to add it to Firefox, click the Add to Firefox button.

With many add-ons that you choose to install, you might see a warning window about the dangers of malicious software or you might have to agree to a license agreement similar to the one shown in Figure 9-10. Read through it and then accept or decline.

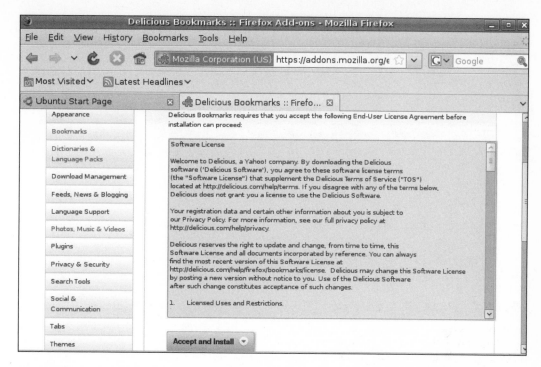

Figure 9-10. *Some add-ons have license agreements for you to accept before installation begins.*

So, what does Delicious do after it's installed? Take a look at Figure 9-11; notice that three new buttons have been added to the toolbar as well as a menu labeled Delicious. The menu is useful, but the Bookmarks button and Add Tag button are what you'll focus on.

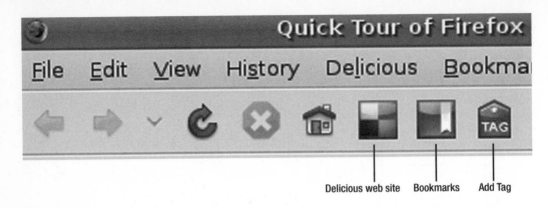

Figure 9-11. *Use the Add Tag button to attach keywords to web sites you bookmark.*

Visit any web site that you visit frequently or want to add to your list of bookmarked web sites. Next, click the Add Tag button; a window appears, similar to the one shown in Figure 9-12.

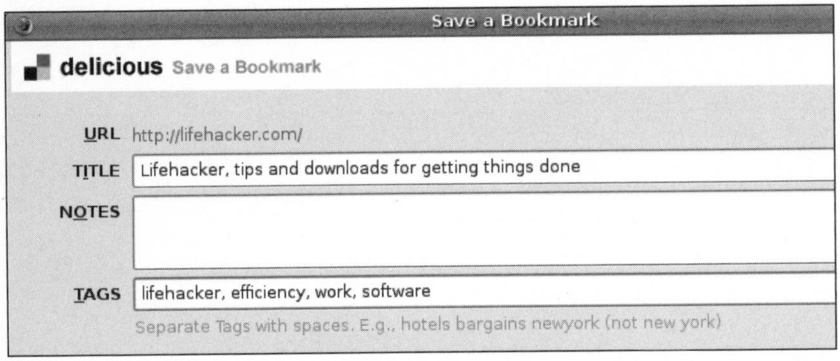

Figure 9-12. *Add tags that can help you later narrow down a search of your bookmarked sites.*

In the Tags text box, enter as many keywords (tags) as you can that describe the web site. In this example, I enjoy visiting `http://www.lifehacker.com` and tagged it with the following tags: **lifehacker**, **efficiency**, **work**, and **software**. Click the Save button when you're finished.

How do tags work? Let's say I visit the Lifehacker blog every day for a year and find various articles that I want to bookmark. By tagging them with **lifehacker** I can now use Delicious to search all my bookmarks for only those web sites that are tagged with lifehacker and nothing else. I do this by clicking the new Delicious Bookmarks button (refer to Figure 9-11) and typing **lifehacker** as my tag in the Bookmarks window to search on, as shown in Figure 9-13.

Figure 9-13. *Searching on keywords filters bookmarked web sites.*

The filtered sites appear at the bottom of the Delicious Bookmarks window; click any web site located in that list, and the page will load in the browser. (You can enter multiple tags to further filter the list.) Click the Delicious Bookmarks button to toggle on and off the filtered list window.

There are add-ons for everything: add-on picture and video viewers, add-on dictionaries and translators, and even add-on eBay monitoring tools (see my list of suggested add-ons at the end of the chapter). Do a keyword search on the Add-ons windows (refer to Figure 9-7) and you're likely to be surprised at the number of add-ons that are being developed and made available to Firefox users.

Configuring the Firefox Homepage

I mentioned earlier that clicking the Homepage button on the toolbar always takes your browser to the web site designated as the homepage. To set your homepage, click the Edit menu and choose Preferences. The Firefox Preferences window opens (see Figure 9-14).

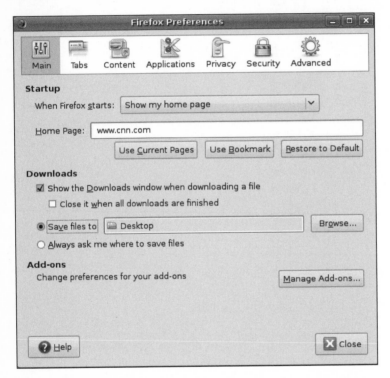

Figure 9-14. *Change the homepage that appears when Firefox opens.*

Enter the web site you want to designate as your homepage in the Home Page text box and click the Close button. I configured http://www.cnn.com as my homepage web site because I always like to read the latest news when I open my web browser.

Deleting Web Browsing History

Many Internet users don't like a history of their browsing kept stored on the computer. Almost all web browsers can erase your browsing history automatically, but it's also easy to manually erase the browsing history. Click the Tools menu and choose the Clear Private Data option (see Figure 9-15).

Figure 9-15. *Use the Tools menu to clear your web browsing history.*

A window opens (see Figure 9-16). You can check and uncheck the various options shown, but if you want to clear your web browsing history, leave the first box in the list checked and click the Clear Private Data Now button.

Figure 9-16. *You can purge browsing history and other stored content.*

Changing the Search Engine

I use Google for my search engine, but I rarely use it for searching book titles. Instead, I prefer to use Amazon.com. But instead of having to visit http://www.amazon.com to search for a book I'm interested in, I can click the downward-pointing arrow indicated in Figure 9-17 and select Amazon.com from the list.

Figure 9-17. *You're not just limited to Google when performing searches.*

I type in my book title or keywords, and my search results will be pulled from Amazon.com's database of books, not the entire Internet that Google would provide. Final results are displayed using whatever search site is selected. Figure 9-18 shows that I'm directed straight to Amazon.com's web site; the search term I entered (**Ubuntu**) is passed along, and a presorted list of possible books is provided. If you do this, don't forget to change the search engine back!

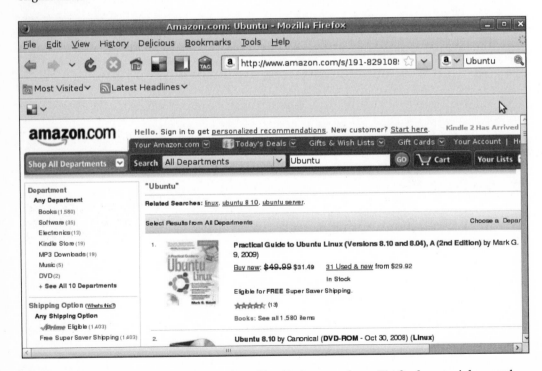

Figure 9-18. *Amazon.com provides me a list of books that match my Firefox browser's keyword.*

Changing the View

Firefox gives you a lot of flexibility when it comes to viewing web sites. Click the View menu, select the Zoom option, and a fly-out menu appears that lets you zoom in and out (see Figure 9-19). I like the Zoom Out feature (which shrinks the page) because I can view a larger piece of the entire web page instead of having to scroll.

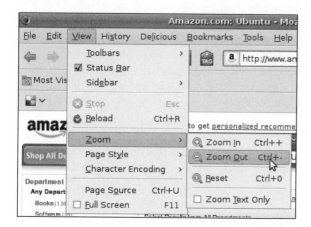

Figure 9-19. *Viewing options include the ability to zoom in and out on a page.*

The View menu also allows you to turn on and off the various toolbars that Firefox provides. For example, in Figure 9-20, I completely turned off the Bookmarks bar and left only the Firefox toolbar; this is done by clicking View, selecting Toolbars, and then unchecking the Bookmarks Toolbar option. I can uncheck the Delicious Toolbar option and provide even more viewing space for web pages; the web site viewing area expands to fill the new space provided.

Figure 9-20. *Turning off a toolbar provides more viewable space for web pages.*

Summarizing Firefox

Firefox is my favorite web browser. Google has released its new Chrome, but it doesn't have the cool add-ons feature that Firefox provides; I like its speed and very simple interface, but I don't think it's quite "there" yet. Microsoft Internet Explorer always seemed to crash on me at various times. And somehow it always managed to catch nasty, malicious software that damaged it and required me to uninstall and reinstall the browser. Thanks, but no thanks. I tried Safari, but it just doesn't compare to my experience with Firefox.

I showed you how to find add-ons and walked you through installing my most-used add-on: Delicious. I have hundreds of bookmarked web pages that I like to go back and revisit, and Delicious doesn't require me to remember the web address. All I need to do is scroll down my list of keywords (visible in Figure 9-13) and I can usually refresh my memory of the keywords that are related to the site I'm looking for. Yes, add-ons are great, and you should spend some time scanning through all the various categories for other useful ones.

At its core, Firefox is a web browser. It comes preinstalled with the Ubuntu operating system installation, so you're ready to go. All the standard features you'll need in a browser can be found in Firefox. Throw in the ability to install add-ons, and you'll probably find that Firefox is your new favorite web browser, too.

Suggested Add-ons for Firefox

Here's a simple list of some add-ons that you might like to download and try with Firefox:

- Block annoying pop-up advertisements with AdBlock Plus: https://addons.mozilla.org/en-US/firefox/addon/1865

- Get a notice when e-mail is delivered to your Gmail account by using Gmail Notifier: https://addons.mozilla.org/en-US/firefox/addon/173

- Quickly find out the current and future weather forecast for your area by installing 1-ClickWeather: https://addons.mozilla.org/en-US/firefox/addon/1035

- Track your packages (UPS, FedEx, DHL) by using the PackageMapping.com Add-on: https://addons.mozilla.org/en-US/firefox/addon/3778

What's Next?

Up next in Chapter 10, I'll introduce you to two of my most favorite applications. I can't live without them! E-mail and a good calendar/scheduling tool are absolute must-haves when it comes to work and personal life. The fact that both of these applications are 100 percent free and simple to use is just icing on the cake. Let's go take a look.

CHAPTER 10

■ ■ ■

Google E-mail and Calendar

While on vacation a few years ago, I received an urgent phone call from a business colleague. He needed a copy of an e-mail that he'd deleted as well as an e-mail address contained in that message. Yes, I did have the e-mail, but unfortunately it was stored on my computer back in my home office—about 350 miles away. After a few hours of phone calls, voice messages, and returned calls, I was able to find someone else who had the original e-mail and was willing to assist.

It made me realize how dependent I had become on my e-mail. All my messages, contacts, and calendar information was stored on my computer's hard drive, and I had no method for accessing it unless I was sitting at my computer. I knew this wasn't an ideal solution.

A few months after this incident, a friend introduced me to Google E-mail, or Gmail. He also showed me Google's Calendar application and how the e-mail and calendar worked together and could be accessed from any computer with Internet connectivity and a web browser. Then he mentioned that Gmail and Calendar were both free to use. I was sold. It took me about one month to transition my e-mail, contacts, and appointments and due dates over to Gmail and Google Calendar, and I've never looked back. By the end of this chapter, you may very well make the same decision I did after seeing these two tools in action.

Welcome to Gmail and Google Calendar

First, the good news: Gmail and Google Calendar are 100 percent free to use. Both services are provided by Google to registered users (more on that shortly). Is there any bad news? Maybe. Google provides these services to you for free and in exchange places small advertisements on the screen when you open an e-mail message. These advertisements are small, are text-only, and never obstruct your view of your e-mail. Take a look at Figure 10-1, which shows an open Gmail message and an advertisement on the right.

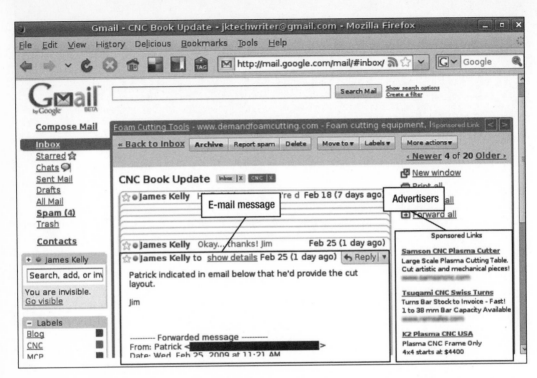

Figure 10-1. *Gmail messages appear in the middle of the screen with advertisements on the right.*

Google Calendar, shown in Figure 10-2, doesn't have any advertisements, but Google could change that at any time. The Calendar offers various views such as a daily or monthly view, and it gives you numerous ways to enter appointments as well as receive reminders; I'll show you how this is done later.

■Note Gmail and Google Calendar don't have version numbers. You don't upgrade these services because there is no software installed on your computer. You're using your web browser to access them, and updates made by Google will be automatically visible to you when you next log on to Gmail or Calendar.

Figure 10-2. *Google Calendar can display events in a monthly view like this or in other views.*

Along the top edge of Figure 10-2, you'll see various links that give you access to Gmail and other Google applications. Documents, for example, gives you access to Google's free online word processor, spreadsheet, and slideshow applications (Google Docs is covered in Chapter 11). Feel free to click these links and see what other free services Google makes available to you.

Before you move on and learn how these two tools are used, however, you'll need to create a Google user account.

Point your web browser to mail.google.com. You should see a screen like the one shown in Figure 10-3.

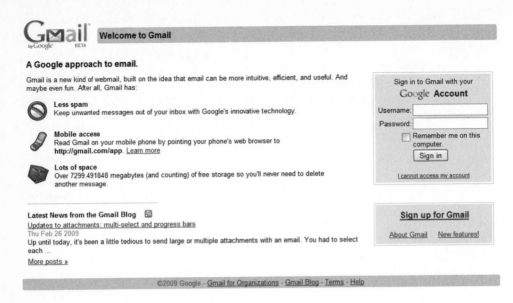

Figure 10-3. *Sign up to use Gmail and Calendar by creating a Google user account.*

Click the "Sign up for Gmail" link and you'll be taken to a screen similar to the one shown in Figure 10-4.

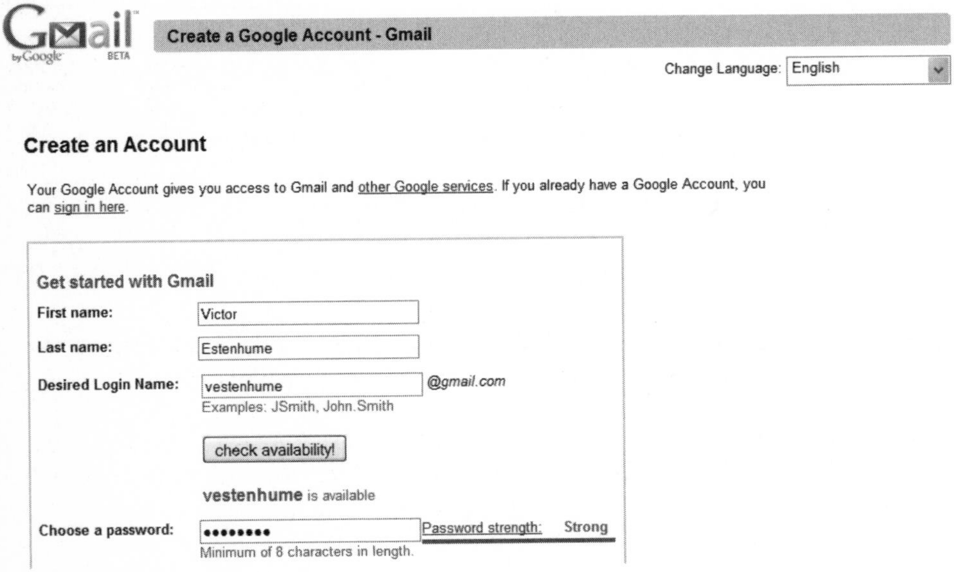

Figure 10-4. *Provide information to create a Google user account.*

You'll be asked to provide your first and last name as well as your desired username (login name). Click the "check availability!" button to make sure that your username is available. If it isn't, try a different one until you get one that isn't taken. Enter a password and reenter the password in the required fields. Be sure to choose a password that Gmail recognizes as a strong password; your password will be given a rating that is visible to the right as you type it. If it's not strong, consider changing it to avoid potential security risks. Complete the remaining tasks on the screen and then click the "I accept. Create my account." button to acknowledge that you've read through the Terms of Service and are ready to start using Gmail and Calendar. Next, click the "I'm ready—show me my account" link in the upper-right corner of the screen.

Gmail will open, and you'll see that a message is waiting for you from the Gmail team, as shown in Figure 10-5. Congratulations! You're a Gmail user (and you have access to Calendar and the other free Google applications, too).

Because you should now have Gmail open and running in a browser window, take a look along the left side of the screen shown in Figure 10-5. You'll see a list of some (hopefully) familiar folders (Inbox, Sent Mail, Drafts, Spam, and Trash) and a few new ones, including Starred and Chats. The (1) next to Inbox shows that one unread message is waiting.

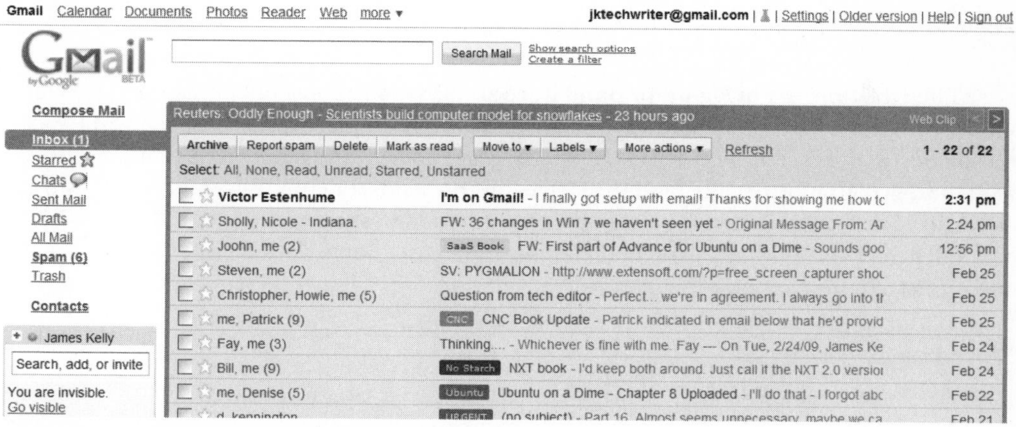

Figure 10-5. *Messages are stored in folders such as Inbox, Spam, and Trash.*

Clicking any of the folders shows any messages stored inside. Messages are displayed to the right of the folder list, and clicking a message opens it for viewing and other options such as replying and forwarding.

Figure 10-6 shows that I've clicked the e-mail from Victor and opened it. I can respond to Victor by simply typing my response in the box below the message and clicking the Send button that appears, but I can also do more than simply reply.

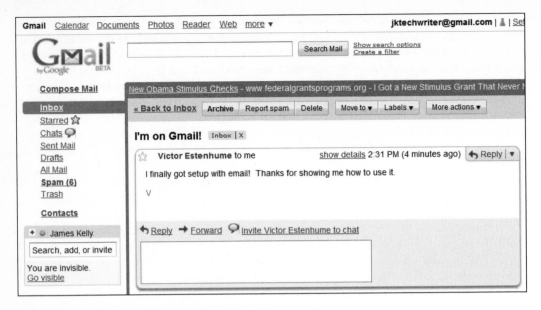

Figure 10-6. *After opening an e-mail, you have many options.*

Along the top edge of Figure 10-6 you'll see six buttons: Archive, "Report spam," Delete, "Move to," Labels, and "More actions." The Archive button sends the message to the All Mail folder, the "Report spam" button sends it to the Spam folder (and blocks that e-mail address from hitting your Inbox again), and the Delete button sends it to the Trash folder. The "Move to," Labels, and "More actions" buttons provide other interesting options that I'll cover shortly.

Click the Reply button shown in the upper-right corner of the e-mail message and you'll see the list of options shown in Figure 10-7.

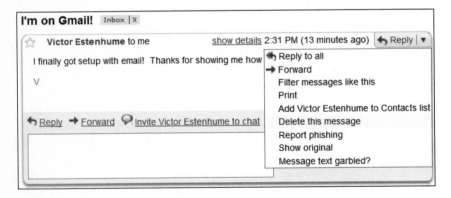

Figure 10-7. *The Reply button offers many options for responding to e-mail.*

Familiar options include Reply, "Reply to all," Forward, Print, and "Delete this message." The "Filter message like this" option is useful (I'll cover it later in the chapter). If the message is an attempt to get you to provide financial or personal information (called *phishing*), click "Report phishing," and Google will investigate the sender.

You can click the Help link in the upper-right corner of the Gmail screen to learn more about any of Gmail's features. I'll be showing you more of Gmail's features later in the chapter, but for now let's take a quick look at Calendar by clicking the Calendar link in the upper-left corner of the screen (refer to Figure 10-6).

When Calendar first opens, it looks like the screen shown in Figure 10-8.

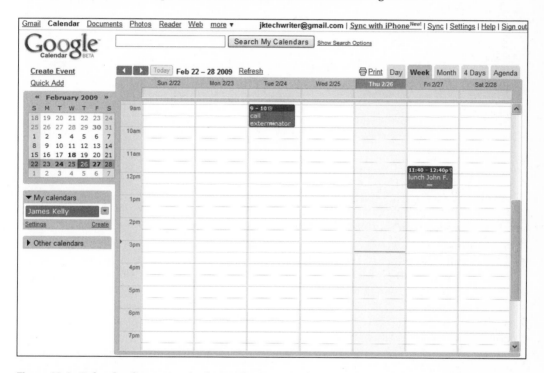

Figure 10-8. *Calendar first opens in the Week view.*

This is called the Week view; it shows the current week displayed in column form. Appointments appear as boxes. You might like this view, but for now, press **M** on your keyboard, and the Calendar will change to the Month view, as shown in Figure 10-9. This is my preferred view and the one I'll be using throughout the chapter.

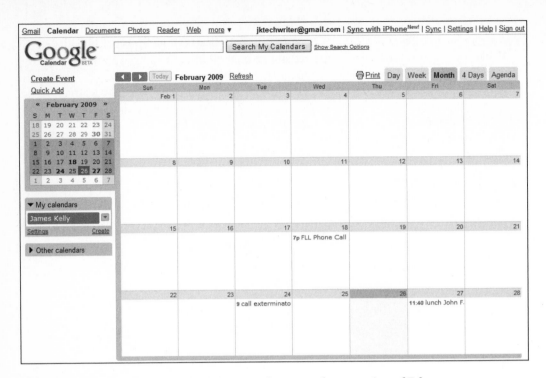

Figure 10-9. *The Month view in Calendar provides a complete overview of February appointments.*

Additional views are Day, 4 Days, and Agenda. Click each of these tabs to see how the calendar is displayed; you might prefer a different view. You can click the left and right arrows indicated in Figure 10-9 to move forward and backward. In this example, one click of the back button allows me to jump back to January 2009, and a single click of the forward button changes the calendar to March 2009.

For most calendar users, the single most important activity is adding appointments (or *events* in Google terminology). You can click the Create Event button indicated in Figure 10-10, type in a description, and provide the starting and ending dates and times. Click the Save button when done; your event will be added to the calendar.

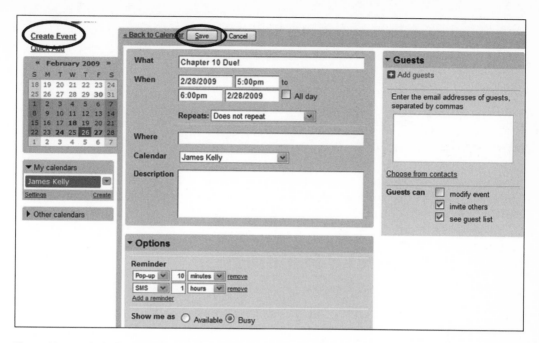

Figure 10-10. *Click the Create Event button to provide details for an appointment.*

A much easier method is to simply click the day (in Month view) or time (in Day or Week view), and a small window appears (see Figure 10-11). In this example, I provide a short description and the time of the event after clicking February 26. I click the Create Event button to finalize the event.

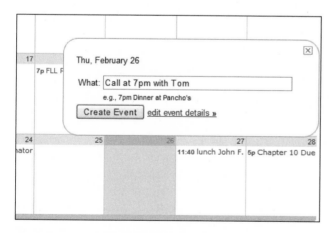

Figure 10-11. *Clicking a specific day allows you to enter a brief description and time.*

My event is added, and Google Calendar is smart enough to figure out from my description the time and will fill in the details (see Figure 10-12).

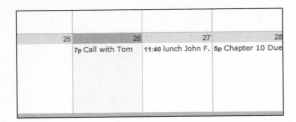

Figure 10-12. *Google Calendar examines the event's details and adds the appointment.*

If that were all there was to Gmail and Google Calendar, you probably wouldn't be too impressed. But these two applications offer much more than simply reading and replying to e-mail and entering appointments. Let's take a look.

Gmail and Calendar Features

Gmail and Calendar have more hidden gems than I could ever hope to cover in a single chapter. The following sections describe some of the most useful features of Gmail and Calendar.

■**Tip** One of my favorite places to learn all kinds of Gmail and Calendar tricks is `http://www.lifehacker.com`. Visit this great blog and do a keyword search using "Gmail" or "Google Calendar" and you'll find dozens of articles that describe hidden features and how to use them.

Organizing E-mail Using Labels

Take a look at Figure 10-13. Notice those small blocks in front of some of the Subject lines? The blocks, which are called *labels*, make organizing and searching for messages extremely simple.

■**Note** I love labels. They're my favorite feature in Gmail—seriously! They're extremely useful for organizing your Inbox. Even better, however, is that you can search your Sent Mail and All Mail folders by using labels. You might be used to using folders with subfolders (and they might contain subfolders), so searching for messages can be a real pain. Not with labels! After a message has a label applied, it can be found quickly, no matter where it's stored. I'll show you how this works in more detail shortly.

You can pick the color and name of each label to make it more visually pleasing. For example, my Urgent label is bright red and makes any e-mail tagged as Urgent difficult to ignore!

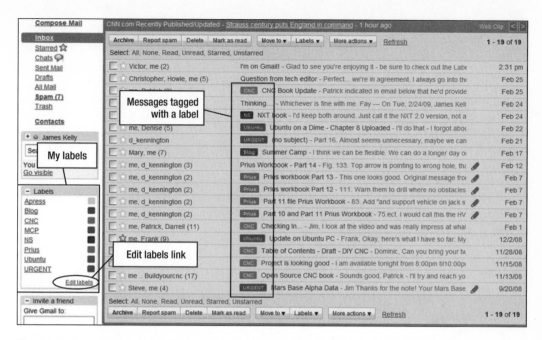

Figure 10-13. *Labels make e-mail easier to organize and search.*

If I click any label on the left side of the screen (refer to Figure 10-13), only the e-mail tagged with that label displays. Figure 10-14 shows that I clicked the CNC label (colored orange) and I can review my message concerning the CNC book without having to dig through hundreds or even thousands of other messages.

CNN.com Recently Published/Updated - *Strauss century puts England in command* - 1 hour ago			Web Clip	< >
Remove label "CNC" Report spam Delete Mark as read Move to ▼ Labels ▼ More actions ▼ Refresh				1 - 9 of 9
Select: All, None, Read, Unread, Starred, Unstarred				
☐ ☆ me, Patrick (9)	CNC Inbox	CNC Book Update - Patrick indicated in email		Feb 25
☐ ☆ me, Patrick, Darrell (11)	CNC Inbox	Checking In... - Jim, I look at the video and wa		Feb 1
☐ ☆ me .. Dominic (6)	CNC	Update CNC book - James, That's great to hear J I ca		12/31/08
☐ ☆ Dominic .. me (6)	CNC	Introductions - Build Your Own CNC - Not a problem! I		12/10/08
☐ ☆ me .. Darrell (5)	CNC	Measurements and materials - I printed out one page 📎		11/29/08
☐ ☆ me .. Dominic (8)	CNC Inbox	Table of Contents - Draft - DIY CNC - Dominic		11/28/08
☐ ☆ me .. Dominic, Darrell (8)	CNC	Update on CNC book - Dominic, I forgot to answer one		11/22/08
☐ ☆ me, Buildyourcnc (4)	CNC Inbox	Project is looking good - I am available tonigh		11/15/08
☐ ☆ me .. Buildyourcnc (17)	CNC Inbox	Open Source CNC book - Sounds good, Patr		11/13/08
Select: All, None, Read, Unread, Starred, Unstarred				
Remove label "CNC" Report spam Delete Mark as read Move to ▼ Labels ▼ More actions ▼ Refresh				1 - 9 of 9

Figure 10-14. *Clicking a label filters out all e-mail not tagged with that label.*

How do you create your own labels? Simple. Click the "Edit labels" button shown in the lower-left corner of Figure 10-13. You see a window similar to the one shown in Figure 10-15.

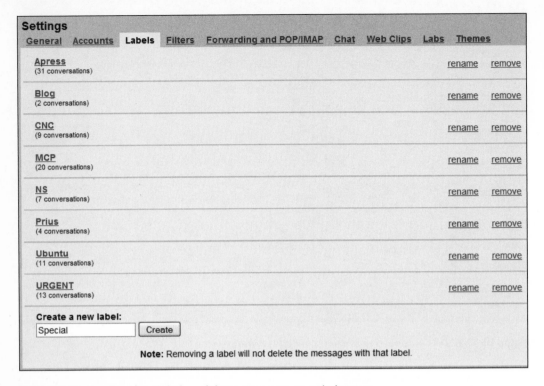

Figure 10-15. *Create a new label, or delete or rename an existing one.*

Enter your label name, as indicated in the figure, and click the Create button; in this example, I'm creating a new label titled Special. Your new label will appear in the list of labels. Click the small colored square to the right of your label to pick a color. Notice also in Figure 10-15 that you can rename or remove an existing label by clicking the appropriate link to the right of any label.

To assign a label to a message, place a check in the box to the left of the message, as shown in Figure 10-16. Click the Labels button and select a label from the drop-down list. An e-mail can have multiple labels, but you must perform this action for each label to be added.

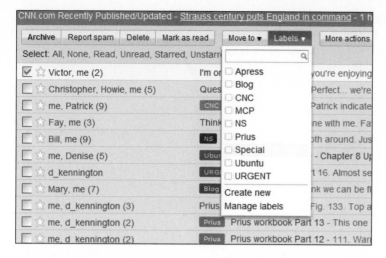

Figure 10-16. *Select a message and use the Labels drop-down list to assign a label.*

Using labels is a great way to make it easier for you to find that "e-mail in a haystack," but the previous steps require you to assign labels after you've received a message. Wouldn't it be great if an incoming message could automatically be tagged with a label of your choice? Well, it can—with another nice feature of Gmail called *Filters*.

Organize E-mail with Filters

I want all incoming e-mail from Apress (the wonderful publisher of this fine book) to be tagged with a bright blue label. To do this, I must first create an Apress label (see preceding section on creating labels). Once that's done, I click the Settings menu and click the Filters tab (see Figure 10-17).

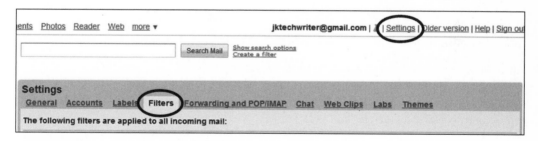

Figure 10-17. *Use the Settings option to access the Filters feature.*

Click "Create a new filter" at the bottom of the page and you'll see a screen like the one shown in Figure 10-18. You can enter someone's e-mail address (or a portion of it, leaving out username@ and leaving just apress.com) in the From field. You can also create filters that search for words in the Subject line or in the actual text of the message. Click the Next Step button when done.

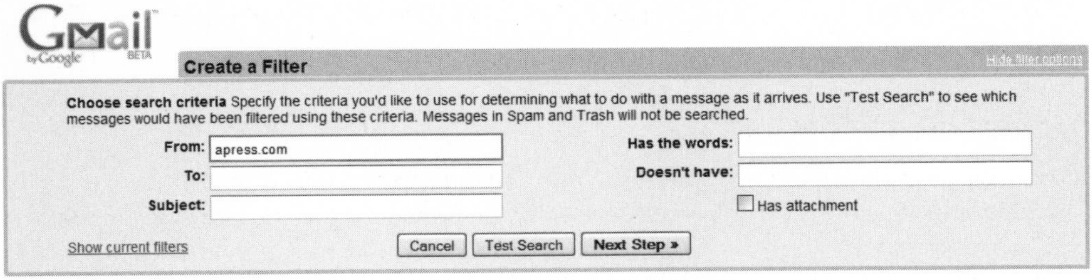

Figure 10-18. *Create a filter using an e-mail address or words that may be in a message.*

On the next screen, shown in Figure 10-19, place a checkmark next to "Apply the label" and select the label from the drop-down list. Click the Create Filter button to finish.

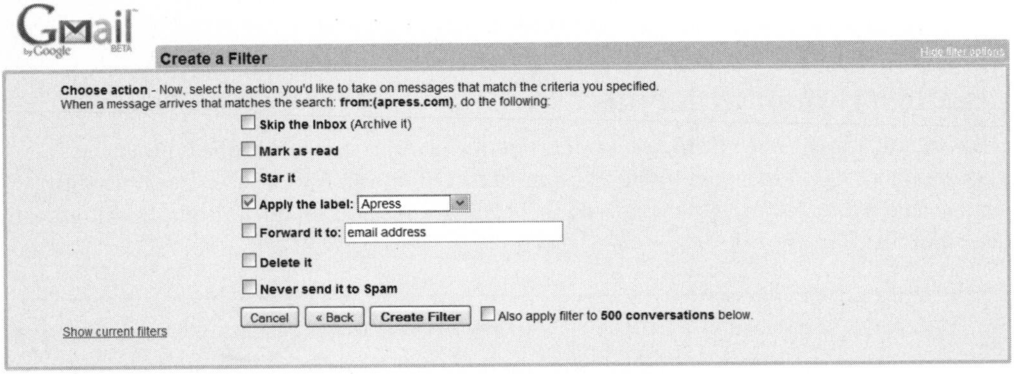

Figure 10-19. *Select the label that will tag any message that matches your new filter.*

Figure 10-20 shows that my new filter is added; I can click the edit link to make changes or remove it by clicking the delete link.

Matches: **from:(apress.com)**
Do this: Apply label "Apress"   edit   delete

Create a new filter

Figure 10-20. *The new filter is turned on, and incoming messages will be checked for matches.*

If any messages come in from anyone at Apress, I'll now see a nice blue Apress label that makes them easier to spot.

Organizing Calendars

Now let's jump to the Calendar application. Your Calendar is available after you log in to Google and (by default) it's visible only to you. Google provides a nice feature, however, that allows you to create multiple calendars (such as a Work calendar and a Home calendar). Again, these calendars are private and visible only to you, but there is a way to make one or more of your calendars viewable by anyone with a web browser. Here's how it's done.

First, open Calendar and click the Settings link in the upper-right corner of the screen (refer to Figure 10-17). The Settings link can be found here on all the Google applications, not just Gmail.

Click the Calendars tab; then click the "Create new calendar" button (see Figure 10-21).

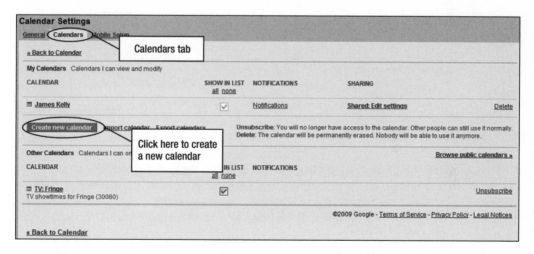

Figure 10-21. *You can create as many additional calendars as you like.*

Provide a calendar name and other information, as shown in Figure 10-22. Notice that you can either make the calendar viewable to everyone (anyone with Internet access and a browser) or you can specify individuals by entering their e-mail addresses at the bottom of the screen.

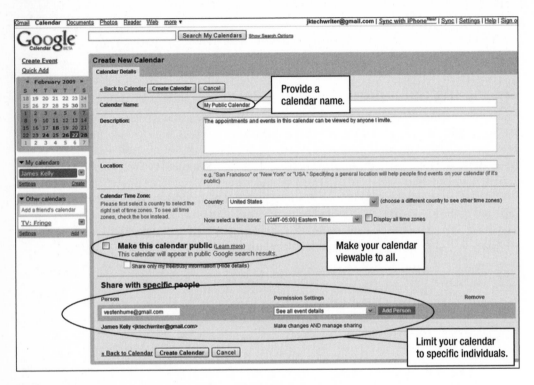

Figure 10-22. *Give your calendar a name and decide who can see it.*

If you provide an e-mail address, click the Add Person button and use the Permission Settings drop-down list to further define what this person can and can't view. A few of the options include "See all event details" and "Make changes to events."

Click the Create Calendar button, and the new calendar will be listed underneath the private calendar (see Figure 10-23).

Figure 10-23. *My Personal Calendar is added to the list of calendars.*

Now, when I add an event to my calendar by clicking a particular date, I have a new Calendar drop-down list, as shown in Figure 10-24. I can select from the list which calendar will contain the event before clicking the Create Event button. Easy!

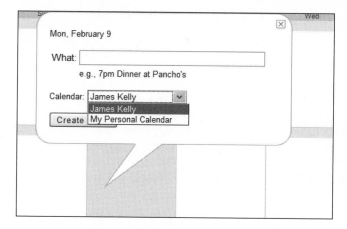

Figure 10-24. *When creating an event, you have to decide which calendar will list the event.*

Calendar Reminders Using Text Messaging

I don't spend every minute of my day in front of my computer, and I'm sure you don't, either. Google Calendar can be configured to send an e-mail reminder to you or pop an alert up on your screen at a preconfigured time. But again this usually requires that you be sitting in front of your computer to see the alert or read the e-mail.

That's why I love that Google Calendar will also send a text message to my mobile phone. If I'm out running errands, I almost always have my mobile phone with me, and getting text message reminders is a great feature. Here's how it works.

First, you need to enable Google Calendar to send you text messages. To do this, click the Settings link in the upper-right corner and then click the Mobile Setup link. You'll see the window shown in Figure 10-25.

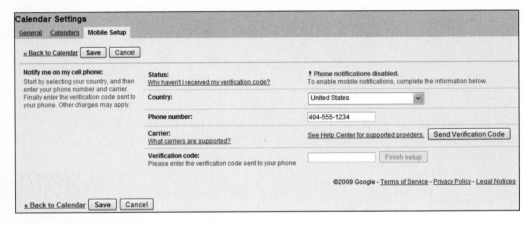

Figure 10-25. *You can enable your mobile phone to receive text messages from Google.*

Enter your mobile phone number in the "Phone number" text box and click the Send Verification Code button. If your mobile phone carrier is supported by Google (most are), you'll receive a test message with a verification code. Enter that code in the "Verification code" text box shown in Figure 10-25, click the "Finish setup" button, and you're ready to start receiving text message alerts.

Now create an event, as shown in Figure 10-26, and click the Create Event button after typing in your description and date/time.

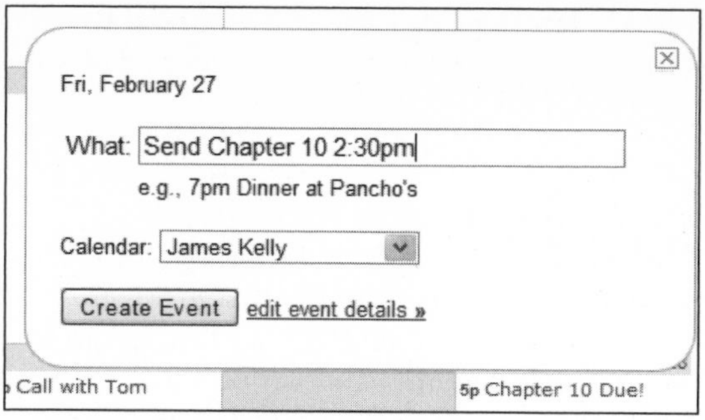

Figure 10-26. *Create an event for which you want to be reminded via a mobile phone text message.*

Next, click on your new event and click the "edit event details" link. Under the Options area of the screen shown in Figure 10-27, click the "Add a reminder" link. A new reminder option called SMS will appear, as shown in Figure 10-27.

■**Note** Two other reminder options are available: Email and Pop-up. Figure 10-27 shows that a pop-up alert will appear 10 minutes prior to the event, and an e-mail will be sent one hour prior to the event. Modify the times as you see fit or click the "remove" link to delete a reminder option.

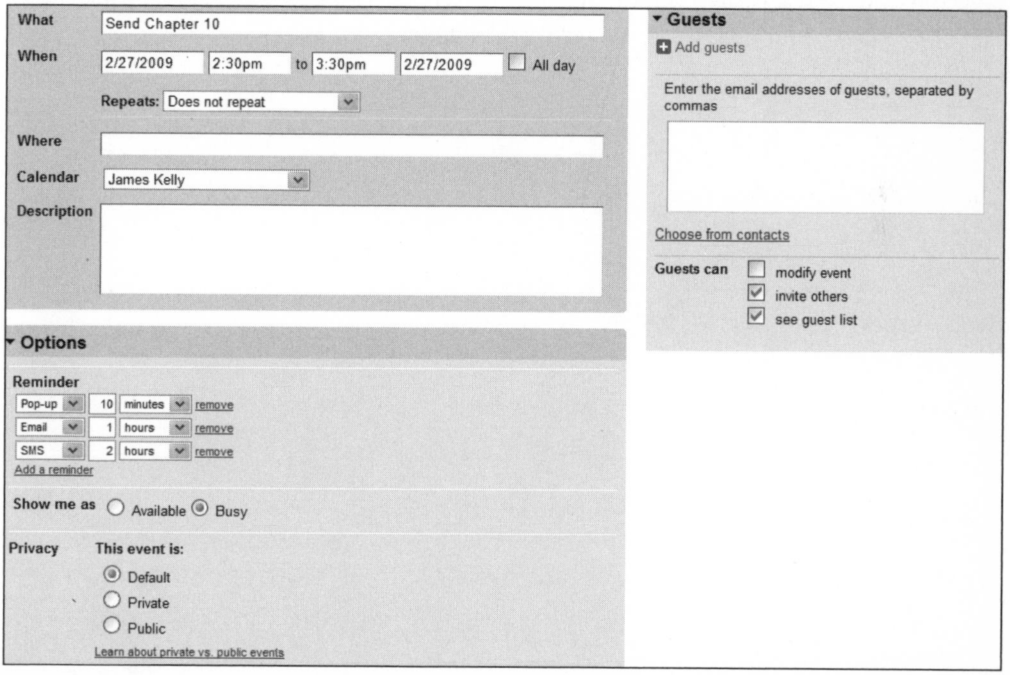

Figure 10-27. *Email and Pop-up alerts are standard, but you can also add a text message alert.*

In this example, I scheduled Google Calendar to send me a text message reminder two hours prior to the actual event. Click the Save button when you're done; a text message alert keeps you from forgetting your appointment.

Summarizing Gmail and Calendar

There are hundreds of web sites and books available that provide more details, more feature coverage, and more tips for using these two applications. That should tell you a little bit about how popular these two tools are; fans of Gmail and Google Calendar are everywhere.

Gmail and Calendar are just two Google applications, but they're among the most popular with users; they're free, easy to use, and make life easier for people who are always on the go. I can't imagine going back to accessing my e-mail and appointments from just one computer. If you're finding yourself in that situation, Gmail and Calendar are a good first step to breaking away and letting Internet access provide you with your e-mail and appointments from any computer with online access.

But don't stop there. Google also offers more free applications that liberate you from using a single computer. What are they?

What's Next?

You just learned about Gmail and Calendar, but I'm guessing that you also occasionally write a letter. Others of you might use a spreadsheet for business (or pleasure—whatever makes you happy). And some of you might need to give an occasional presentation at school, work, or event. Well, you'll be pleased to know that Google has a solution for each of those needs. It's called Google Docs, and Chapter 11 will tell you all about it.

CHAPTER 11

■■■

Google Documents

Today, it's almost impossible to purchase a new computer without finding a preinstalled *productivity suite* installed. And by *productivity*, I'm talking about a collection of software that typically includes a word processor, a spreadsheet, an e-mail/calendar app and some-times a slideshow application, so it is sometimes also referred to as an *office suite*. If you installed Ubuntu on your U-PC, the OpenOffice.org office suite is already installed.

Earlier in the book, I introduced you to the OpenOffice.org office suite that consists of Writer, Calc, and Impress (refer to Chapters 5, 6, and 7, respectively). OpenOffice is an excep-tional office suite that is 100 percent free to *download and install* (note the emphasis), but it's not the only free office suite. Google also has an office suite that is growing in popularity and offers some really nice features. Why am I including another office suite chapter when OpenOffice comes so highly recommended? Simple—because Google's office suite requires no download or installation of any software, and the tools are always available from any online computer's web browser. That's why I like Google's solution.

But it's not the only difference, as you'll soon see; by the end of this chapter, you'll have enough information to decide which of the two office suites will most meet your needs. You might even find yourself using both, as I do, depending on your circumstances and the job at hand.

Welcome to Google Docs

OpenOffice.org isn't the only organization to offer a free office suite. Google has entered the arena with its own collection of applications called Google Documents—Google Docs for short.

Google Docs is accessed through your web browser. After logging in to any Google service (such as Gmail or Google Calendar, covered in Chapter 10), click the Documents link in the top-right corner of the page, as shown in Figure 11-1. The screen shown in this figure is the Google Docs main page. From this page, you can create new documents such as a spreadsheet or slideshow, edit or delete existing documents, create folders to organize documents, and more.

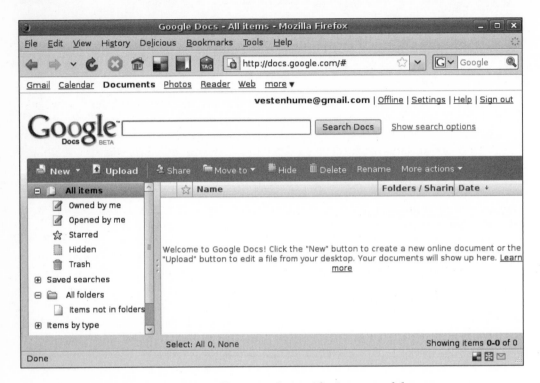

Figure 11-1. *Google Docs is an online office suite that resides in your web browser.*

Google Docs has a simple user toolbar (see Figure 11-2).

Figure 11-2. *Google Docs' toolbar doesn't complicate things with hundreds of options.*

Feel free to click the New, "Move to," and "More actions" drop-down menus to see what's available. You'll see some of these menus and buttons used later in the chapter.

Figure 11-3 shows the left side of the screen, in which Google Docs lists folder locations. Google Docs doesn't limit you to its preconfigured folders; you can create your own subfolders to help you organize your projects and documents. In this example, I created a folder of my own Not So Secret Projects, listed under "All folders."

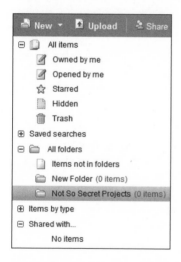

Figure 11-3. *Google Docs uses a simple folder hierarchy for organizing documents.*

To create your own folders, click the New menu, select Folders, and provide a name. Click the Save button when done, and your new folder will be added under "All folders." (Note also in Figure 11-3 the two folders called "Owned by me" and "Shared with." They will be covered later in the chapter, but I hope you're seeing a hint of a feature offered by Google Docs.)

Finally, the majority of the Google Docs main page is taken up with displaying documents. Figure 11-4 shows three documents created by me: a presentation titled How to Fix a Flat, a spreadsheet titled Recipe Ingredient Tests, and a word processing document titled Super Secret Book Proposal. I click a document to open it or place a check in the box beside its name and to select an option on the toolbar (such as Delete or Rename).

Figure 11-4. *Documents are listed on the right side of the main page.*

Because my documents are stored with Google Docs, I can access these files from any computer with Internet access and a web browser. Think about it—I no longer need be a prisoner to my home office when I want to work on a file. I don't even have to carry my laptop with me when I travel; as long as I know I'll have a web browser with an Internet connection where I'm going, I can access my documents by logging into Google Docs and using its tools.

■**Caution** Word processing documents, spreadsheets, and other files created using Google Docs are not always 100 percent compatible with applications such as Microsoft Word or Excel (or vice versa). Even though Google Docs will allow you to save documents in "standard" formats, you should always verify that a file can be opened properly with any other applications you anticipate the file might be opened, edited, or printed with.

Now, don't laugh; Google's marketing department didn't spend a fortune coming up with clever names for its office suite tools. For its word processor, the application is called Document. Take a guess what it calls its spreadsheet application? Yep: Spreadsheet. And its slideshow tool goes by the impressive moniker of Presentation. (I told you not to laugh.)

But ignoring the simplistic names, these three tools do exactly what their names describe: you use them to create a document, spreadsheet, or presentation.

To create a word processing document, click the New button and choose Document. Figure 11-5 shows a blank Document file.

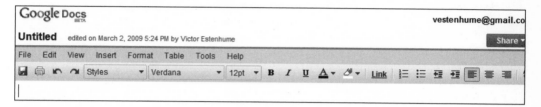

Figure 11-5. *Google Docs offers Document as its word processing application.*

Spend some time clicking the various menus and seeing which options are available. The toolbar contains a minimum number of buttons, but somehow Google has managed to provide just what I need and nothing more. Another feature I like is the large blank document screen; the absence of screen clutter can be a shock at first, but you'll come to enjoy it.

Tip Be sure to click the Save button in the upper-right corner often; Google has made it extremely easy and fast to locate, so there's no excuse for accidentally losing any of your work. Likewise, instead of clicking the File menu and choosing Close, simply click the Save & Close button and you can save your work and exit Document at once.

To open a new spreadsheet, click the New button on the Google Docs main page and select Spreadsheet. Figure 11-6 shows a blank Spreadsheet worksheet.

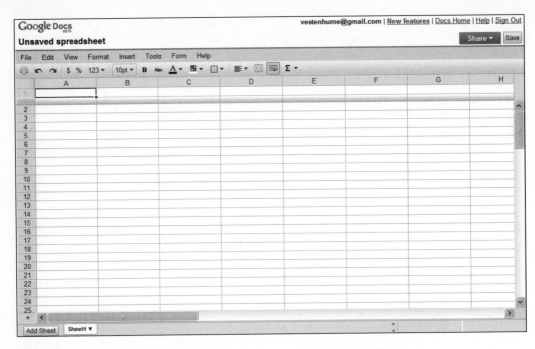

Figure 11-6. *Spreadsheet is Google Docs' answer to a spreadsheet application.*

Google Docs Spreadsheet works like every other spreadsheet you've probably used before; click the Help menu if you're unfamiliar with using a spreadsheet; Google Docs will provide you with plenty of assistance if you select the Google Docs Help Center option.

Note For some reason, Spreadsheet does not have a Save & Close button like Document. To close your worksheet, click the File menu and choose Save & Close.

Finally, to create a new slideshow, click the New button and select Presentation. A blank slideshow file will open, as shown in Figure 11-7.

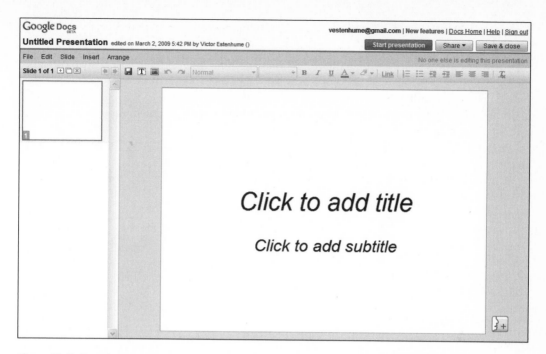

Figure 11-7. *Google Docs Presentation allows you to create your own slideshows.*

As you add slides to your presentation, a thumbnail view of each slide will appear in the left column. Clicking a slide thumbnail will display the larger slide to the right, in which you can enter text, video, pictures, and formatting.

A single chapter can't do justice to providing you with complete instructions on using Document, Spreadsheet, and Presentation. But my purpose for this chapter isn't to show you how to use these three applications; instead, I want to demonstrate what I believe is the real power available when you use Google Docs: sharing your files with the world, a group, or a single individual, and collaborating on a document with other Google Docs users. (Google Docs provides complete online documentation for using all three tools if you click the Help link in the upper-right corner of the screen.)

Working with Google Docs

If you never plan to publish or collaborate on any files you create with Google Docs with another person, feel free to skip this section. But you'll be missing out on what I consider to be one of the real advantages of using Google Docs (the other being mobility and accessing your files from any online computer). Here's how collaboration and publishing work.

Collaborating with Google Docs

Maybe you've spent months or years writing that 900-page Great American Novel and are ready to get some opinions from a friend or family member. You might just as likely have created the perfect spreadsheet that helps a new car buyer fill in all the numbers to calculate her monthly payment and you want to share it with the world. Or maybe you're like me and have given some presentations in the past and received e-mail from audience members requesting a copy of the slideshow. Well, Google Docs makes it extremely easy to share your work with a single person, a group, or the world at large. And it all starts by opening the file you want to share.

Figure 11-8 shows one of my Document files titled Super Secret Book Proposal (the following steps also work for Spreadsheet and Presentation files).

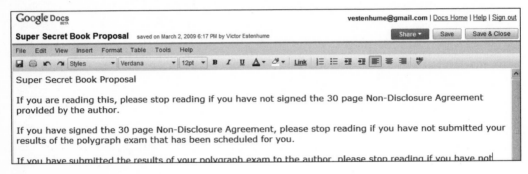

Figure 11-8. *Calendar first opens in the Week view.*

Click the Share button in the upper-right corner of the screen and you'll see a list of options (see Figure 11-9).

Figure 11-9. *The Share button offers numerous sharing options for the document.*

The second option in the list, "Email as attachment," is fairly self-explanatory; your document will be sent out using your Gmail account to any e-mail addresses you specify in the pop-up window. You can also enter a message to the recipients, just like a regular e-mail message.

Click the first option, "Share with others," and a window will open (see Figure 11-10).

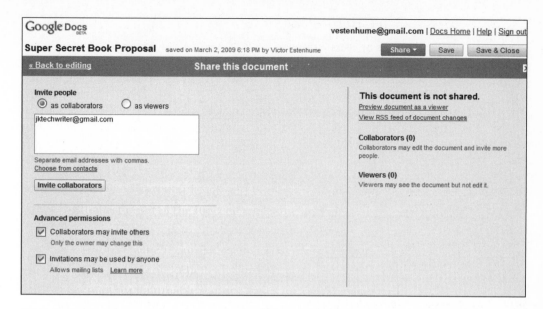

Figure 11-10. *You can share the document and grant privileges such as the ability to view or edit.*

Notice in the upper-left portion of the screen that anyone you choose to share your document with will be designated as either a collaborator or a viewer. Collaborators can edit the document and even invite other collaborators. I'll go into more detail on how this works in the next section.

Viewers can only read a document or presentation or spreadsheet. Any changes a viewer attempts to make to the open document will be unsuccessful.

Because the focus in this section is collaborating with other users, you'll leave "as collaborators" selected. (For those who you want to allow only viewing privileges, select "as viewers" and perform the same steps described as follows—just keep in mind that viewers will not be allowed to make changes to your documents.) Type in the e-mail addresses of those you want to give collaboration privileges in the box, as shown in Figure 11-10. In this example, I entered jktechwriter@gmail.com.

You'll also want to consider the two Advanced permissions available as check boxes in the lower-left corner—"Collaborators may invite others" and "Invitations may be used by anyone"—which will allow you or any collaborator to invite an entire mailing list. By default, both boxes are checked, so uncheck any option that doesn't meet your goals. (For example, if you want only one collaborator to provide feedback and changes for your new book, uncheck both boxes and prevent that person from allowing anyone else to possibly view it.)

After you enter one or more e-mail addresses and verify the Advanced permissions you want to give or revoke, click the "Invite collaborators" button. You'll see a window open (see Figure 11-11).

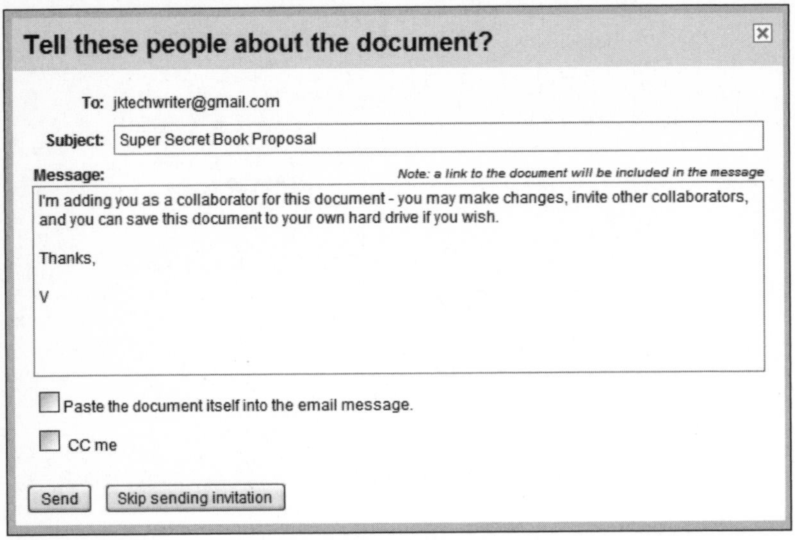

Tell these people about the document?   ☒

To: jktechwriter@gmail.com

Subject: Super Secret Book Proposal

Message: *Note: a link to the document will be included in the message*

I'm adding you as a collaborator for this document - you may make changes, invite other collaborators, and you can save this document to your own hard drive if you wish.

Thanks,

V

☐ Paste the document itself into the email message.

☐ CC me

[Send]   [Skip sending invitation]

Figure 11-11. *It can be helpful to tell your invitees that they have access to a document.*

Enter a brief (or detailed) message to the invitee(s) and click the Send button. Each invitee will receive an e-mail, notifying them that they have collaborator or viewer status for your document and a link directly to the document.

As you add collaborators (or viewers), the list on the right side of the screen shown in Figure 11-12 shows those persons. Click the *x* on the right of any name to remove it as a collaborator or viewer.

Google Docs BETA   vestenhume@gmail.com | Docs Home | Help | Sign out

Super Secret Book Proposal saved on March 2, 2009 6:18 PM by Victor Estenhume   [Share ▾] [Save] [Save & Close]

« Back to editing   **Share this document**   ☒

Invite people   **This document is currently shared.**
◉ as collaborators   ○ as viewers   ✉ Email everyone
                                               ▦ Create event with everyone
                                               Preview document as a viewer
                                               View RSS feed of document changes

Separate email addresses with commas.   **Collaborators (2)** - remove all
Choose from contacts   Collaborators may edit the document.
[Invite collaborators]   Me - owner
                                                 Jktechwriter ☒
                                               ✉ Email collaborators
                                               ▦ Create event with collaborators

Advanced permissions

☐ Collaborators may invite others   **Viewers (1)** - remove all
   Only the owner may change this   Viewers may see the document but not edit it.
                                                 Jim   ☒
☐ Invitations may be used by anyone   ✉ Email viewers
   Allows mailing lists Learn more   ▦ Create event with viewers

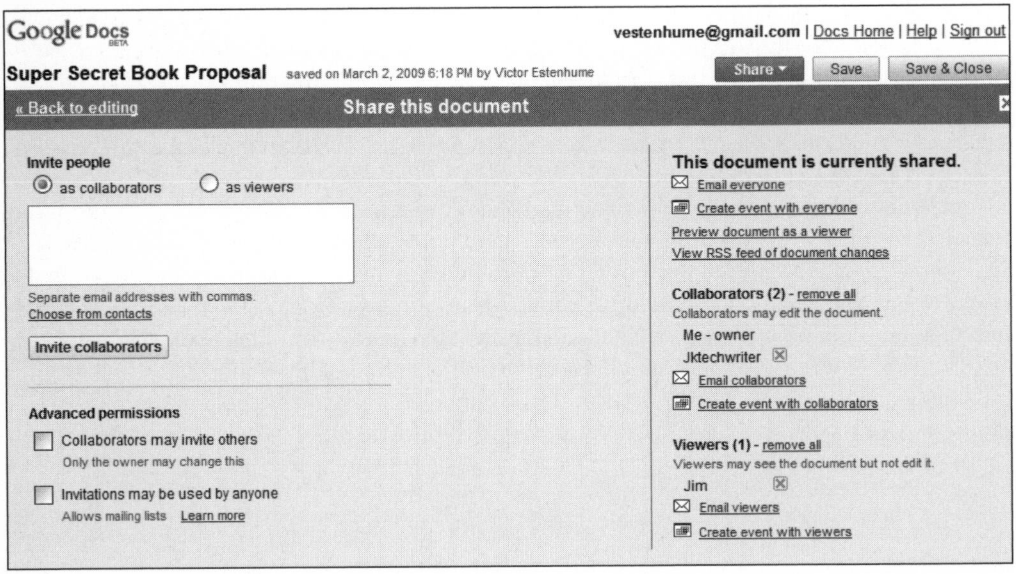

Figure 11-12. *Collaborators and viewers are listed and can be easily deleted.*

A collaborator can open and edit the document at this point. If you have the document open at the same time, you'll see an alert in the lower-right corner of the screen that tells you who else is viewing or editing your document (see Figure 11-13).

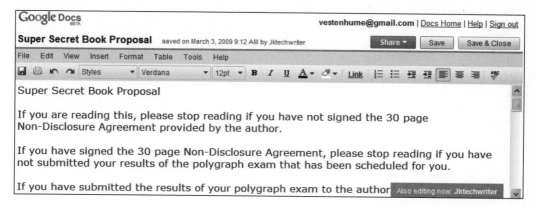

Figure 11-13. *Google Docs alerts you to anyone else viewing or editing your open document.*

Suppose that both of you make changes to the document. Which changes get saved? Google Docs autosaves frequently, and a timestamp is added to the right of the document name (refer to Figure 11-13). This timestamp also lists the name of the last person to make changes. Whomever makes the last change to the document will have their changes saved; that is, until someone else modifies the document. This can be frustrating if you are editing a document simultaneously, which is why Google Docs lets you know when other users are editing and who made the last saved changes.

With Document and Presentation, anyone viewing or editing a document simultaneously is listed (refer to Figure 11-13), and care must be taken to not overwrite one another's edits. But Spreadsheet has one nice feature that I'm hopeful Google Docs will implement soon with the other two applications: a chat window.

When editing a spreadsheet simultaneously, click the other user's name. A chat window opens along the right side of the screen, as shown in Figure 11-14. This is useful for discussing changes to the spreadsheet before making them.

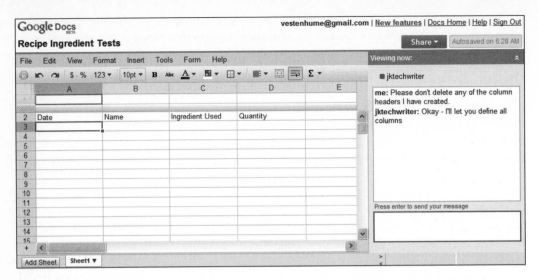

Figure 11-14. *A chat discussion within a spreadsheet window is useful for collaborating.*

Earlier in the chapter I mentioned that you have numerous folders on the Google Docs main page. Take a look at it now, and you should see the names of those who have either collaborator or viewing privileges following each document name (see Figure 11-15). This is a helpful reminder of who is accessing your files.

Figure 11-15. *Those with collaborator or viewing privileges are listed after each document name.*

As you can see, allowing a select group of others to edit or view your document isn't difficult to implement. Google Docs makes it simple to define whether a person can edit or view a document. But what if you want to share a document with everyone—and by everyone, I mean making it viewable (not editable) to anyone with Internet access and a web browser? Well, Google Docs calls that publishing, and here's how it's done.

Publishing a Document

After you create a document, whether it be a spreadsheet, slideshow, or text file, Google Docs makes it extremely simple for you to share it with the world. Google Docs converts the document into a web page with its own address that can be typed in a web browser, e-mailed as a link, or posted in a discussion forum.

To do this, first open the document. In this example, I'll share a Presentation document I created. Click the Share button in the upper-right corner of the screen and select the Publish option.

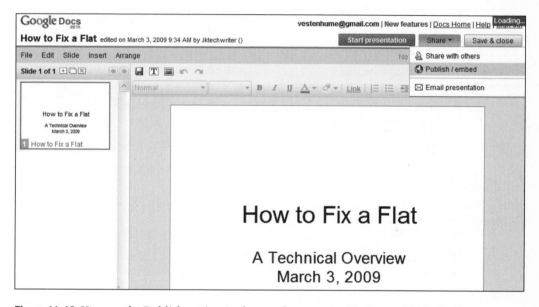

Figure 11-16. *You use the Publish option to share a document with the world via the Internet.*

A window will open, similar to the one shown in Figure 11-17.

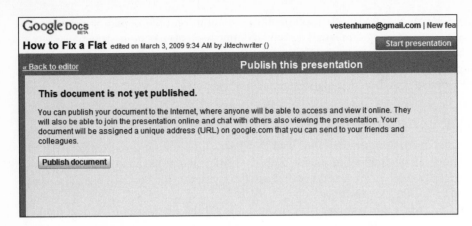

Figure 11-17. *Publishing a document creates a unique web address for the file.*

Click the "Publish document" button shown in Figure 11-17 and you will be provided a URL (see Figure 11-18).

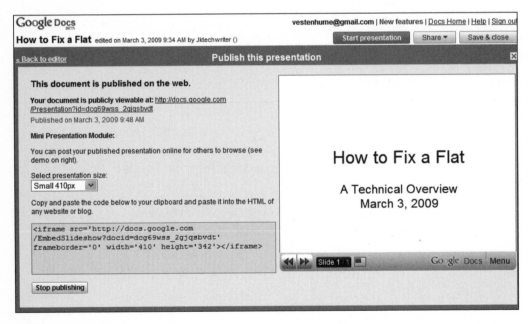

Figure 11-18. *Google Docs provides the HTML code needed to share your document on your blog or web site.*

As seen in Figure 11-18, Google Docs provides numerous options, depending on the type of document being shared. At the top of the screen you'll find the web address that can be e-mailed or posted on a web forum to point viewers to the slideshow. Below the web address, I can choose the size that my presentation will be displayed (Small, Medium, or Large). I can also copy the HTML code at the bottom of the screen and paste it into any web page; the presentation will be visible on that page. The right side of the screen shows a preview of what viewers will see when they view the document.

Finally, I can also click the "Stop publishing" button at any time to remove the document from the public domain.

For Document files, the Publishing options include the ability to post the document on a blog. If you have a blog, click the "Post to blog" button, provide your credentials such as username and password, and click the OK button to have the Document file posted to your blog. (Visit http://www.blogger.com for more information on blogs as well as how to create your own free blog.)

Publishing Spreadsheet files provides an option allowing you to display all worksheets or just worksheet 1. (Although spreadsheets can have multiple worksheets, unfortunately your only choices are All or Sheet 1.)

Summarizing Google Documents

Google Docs provides you with fully functional word processor, spreadsheet, and slideshow applications. I won't pretend that they're feature-heavy and have every special option that you'll need, but they do work in a pinch, and the ability to access your Google Docs files from any web browser, combined with the sharing and collaboration features, is growing the Google Docs user base. This, in turn, is pushing Google to continually update Google Docs with new features that users request. (Be on the lookout for the New Feature link that sometimes appears in the upper-right corner of any Google Docs page you are on; click it and you can read about new options available to you). To submit your own request, click the Help link in the upper-right corner of the main page and then click the Suggestions link on the right side of the screen (see Figure 11-19). Let Google know what you like, dislike, and would love to see added with respect to Google Docs.

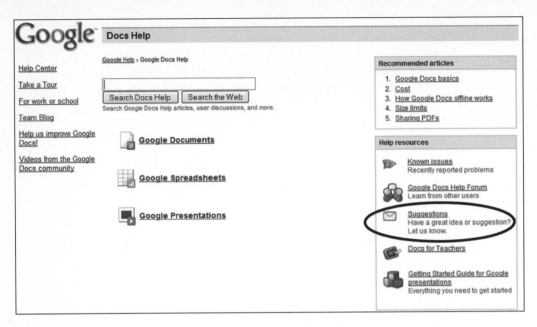

Figure 11-19. *Google Docs provides many options for sharing a document.*

So now you can compare the OpenOffice.org office suite to Google Docs and decide which you prefer to use. If you want to reduce the number of applications installed on your computer, Google Docs is for you. Combine it with Gmail and Calendar (see Chapter 10) and you'll have one lean machine when it comes to installed software!

What's Next?

You're almost done with the book! Chapter 12 will cover the remaining free applications that come preinstalled with Ubuntu as well as some other free applications that might be of interest to you.

■■■

More Apps to Consider

Many of the applications covered in previous chapters are included when you install Ubuntu on your U-PC, but some are not. I've attempted to provide you with overviews of what I believe will be the applications you'll most likely use while running Ubuntu, but there are so many more. This chapter provides brief overviews of additional applications that come with the Ubuntu installation.

In addition to the applications mentioned in this chapter, I'll also include some web sites that cover Ubuntu software developments and other web sites that are simply useful libraries of existing Ubuntu-compatible apps for you to try. So, in no particular order, let's take a look at what else is out there for your U-PC.

Additional Preinstalled Apps

This section explains some of the other apps and tools that you get with the basic Ubuntu installation. No added downloads are required.

Calculator

Every operating system seems to have a calculator app, and Ubuntu is no exception. Click the Applications menu, and you'll find the Calculator under the Accessories group. The calculator has four different modes: Basic, Advanced, Financial, and Scientific. Switch between modes using the View menu on the calendar. Figure 12-1 shows the calculator in Scientific mode.

Figure 12-1. *The Ubuntu calculator is a standard accessory.*

Text Editor

Sometimes you don't need all the fancy fonts and options that OpenOffice Writer or Google Docs Document provides. When you find that you just need to create a simple text document (saved with the .txt file extension), click the Applications menu and select Text Editor from the Accessories group (in techspeak, this application is called gedit). You'll be happy to hear, however, that this Text Editor comes with a built-in spell checker that many simple text editors do not provide. Figure 12-2 shows the Text Editor with its simple toolbar interface.

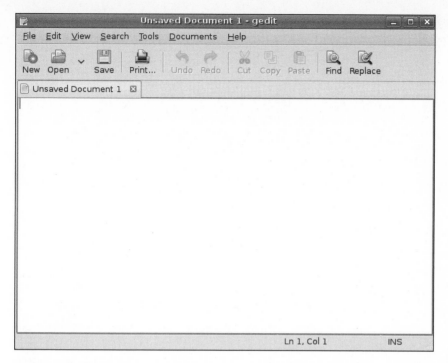

Figure 12-2. *The Text Editor saves files in the .txt file format and has a spell checker.*

Tomboy Notes

A tool that you might find interesting is Tomboy Notes. Click the Applications menu and choose Tomboy Notes from the Accessories Group. Figure 12-3 shows the window that will open.

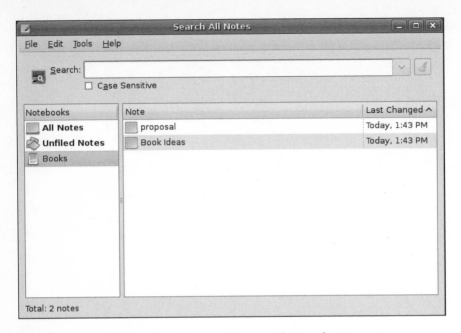

Figure 12-3. *Tomboy Notes lets you organize your ideas and notes.*

It's easy to figure out, but in a nutshell, click the File menu and select New Notebook from the Notebooks group. Give it a title and click the Create button. Your notebook will appear in the left column. In this example, I created a new notebook titled Books. Next, click the File menu and choose New. A blank note will open; click the blue text to rename the title and type your note. Figure 12-4 shows my new note.

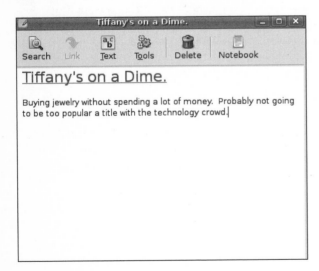

Figure 12-4. *Give your note a title and enter your comments below.*

Click the Notebook button at the top of the note and select the notebook in which it will be stored. Figure 12-5 shows that I placed this note under my Books notebook. Double-click a note to read it, modify it, or delete it. I also created my To Do List to hold any urgent tasks (from my wife) or semiurgent tasks.

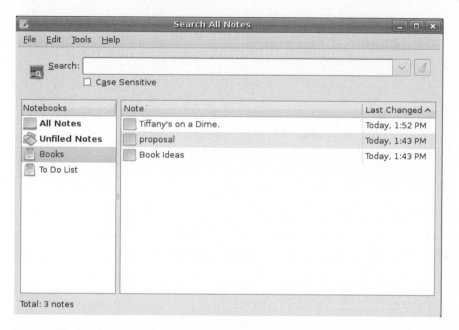

Figure 12-5. *Tomboy Notes lets you organize your notes into notebooks.*

There are many more options that Tomboy Notes provides, including using built-in hyperlinks within notes that will let you jump from note to note with a single click. This is useful if you have a lot of related notes that need to be kept separate but have shared content with other notes. Tomboy Notes also provides the ability to search through all your notes for keywords, as well as print and export notes to HTML.

Brasero Disc Burning

If your U-PC has a CD-RW or DVD-RW (capable of reading and writing to discs), you'll want to check out Brasero, which lets you copy CDs/DVDs or write music or data to discs. If you download any image files (.ISO format), Brasero can also burn (write) that image to a disc for you.

■Note When you purchase software in a box, you get one or more CDs or DVDs that are used to install the application. But when it comes to free software, especially Ubuntu, the free offering is often available only as a download; you'll have to pay to have an installation disc sent to you (see Appendix B). To get around this, many software developers offer the .ISO image file as a way to create your own installation disc(s). Brasero will easily let you create your own installation file: download the .ISO file and click the Burn image button (see Figure 12-6). Follow the instructions, and the installation disc will be burned quickly.

Click the Applications menu and select Brasero Disc Burning from the Sound & Video group to open the application. Figure 12-6 shows Brasero's simple interface. Insert a blank CD-RW or DVD-RW disc, click the appropriate button (such as "Audio project" to make a music CD for playing in your car), and follow the onscreen instructions. Brasero is fast because it's a no-frills burning application. I rarely use any other burning software these days because Brasero is so easy to use.

Figure 12-6. *Brasero provides CD- and DVD-burning capabilities.*

Totem Movie Player

Your U-PC has a built-in DVD player that can be accessed by clicking the Applications menu and selecting Totem Movie Player from the Sound & Video group. The application will open, as shown in Figure 12-7.

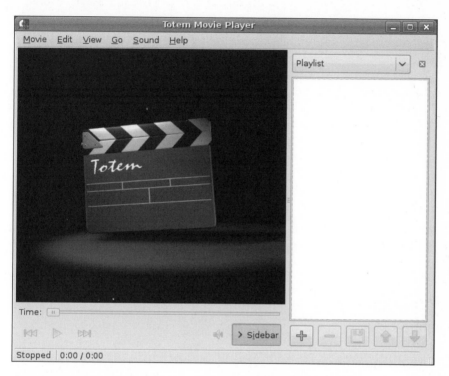

Figure 12-7. *Totem Movie Player can play DVDs as well as movies.*

Insert your DVD (or click the Movie menu and choose Open to browse to the location of any movie files stored on your hard drive). Use the Go menu as you would a remote control: select menu options such as chapter selection, pause, rewind, and more.

Tip If you're having difficulty getting Totem to play a movie, visit https://help.ubuntu.com/ community/RestrictedFormats and follow the instructions for your specific version of Ubuntu. A handful of video file types are "turned off" during the initial install, but this is not a bug in your operating system. To avoid licensing and legal issues with respect to certain proprietary technologies, the Ubuntu developers require you, as the end user of the operating system, to "turn on" support for some media types.

Rhythmbox Music Player

In addition to watching movies on your U-PC, you can also listen to your music CDs and mp3 music files that are stored on your hard drive. Click the Applications menu and select Rhythmbox Music Player from the Sound & Video group. The application will open, as shown in Figure 12-8.

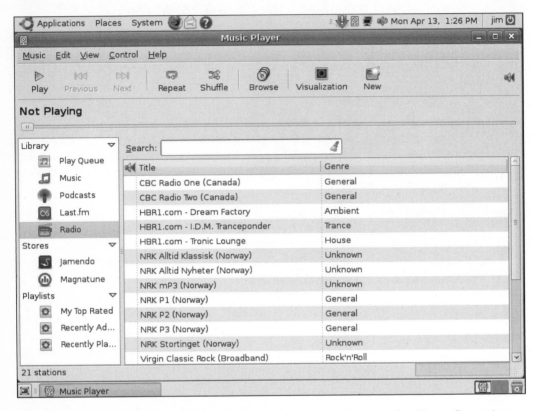

Figure 12-8. *Rhythmbox Music Player lets you listen to CDs, podcasts, and online radio stations.*

If you insert a music CD into the CD/DVD drive, Rhythmbox will detect the disc and list the titles in the center window. You can click the Play button at the top to start playing the CD as well as use the Previous and Next buttons to select the song to play.

Besides playing CDs, you can also listen to other sources (such as podcasts and online radio stations) by selecting the desired option in the left pane. Figure 12-8 shows that I selected the Radio option, and a list of online radio stations are listed in the center window. Double-click a radio station to access and listen to it.

Ubuntu Application Resources

The Internet is both a blessing and a curse when it comes to finding applications for your computer. There are simply so many web sites to sift through to find those diamonds in the rough. Although I can't point you to every great Ubuntu application out there, I can provide you with some web sites that make a good attempt. Hopefully this list will get you pointed in the right direction when you choose to expand the applications installed on your U-PC:

- http://ubuntulinuxhelp.com/top-100-of-the-best-useful-opensource-applications/: Can you go wrong with a list titled "Top 100 of the Best (Useful) OpenSource Applications?" The list breaks down applications by category (such as Audio and Productivity), so be sure to scroll through it and see what's there. I already found a dozen or more that I downloaded and installed.

- http://ubuntuapplications.blogspot.com/2007/08/top-26-ubuntu-application-sources.html: A sort of list of lists, this web site contains 26 of the best web sites for finding Ubuntu-compatible applications. (I told you that there were too many Ubuntu-related web sites to sift through, but these are some of the best you can find, so be sure to bookmark the page.)

- http://www.emmaalvarez.com/2007/12/top-best-50-ubuntu-opensource.html: If you're a software developer, graphic artist, animator, web designer, or a dabbler in any kind of design work using your computer, the "Top 50 Ubuntu OpenSource Applications for Design and Development" list is for you. It provides 2D, 3D, and animation software links that work great with Ubuntu.

- http://ubuntulinuxhelp.com/top-12-best-games-for-ubuntu-linux-1-tremulous/: This link will take you to the first of 12 games that have been described as the best games for Ubuntu. After you tire of Solitaire, Blackjack, and Mines, try your hand at one or more of these games and see that great games do exist for Ubuntu, not just Windows. (Grid-wars is my favorite—I play it way too much. If you're a child of the 1980s, this game will bring back many memories.)

- http://www.freebrowsergamer.com/: If you want to play some games without installing any software (or taking up any more of your valued hard drive space), check out this site for free games that can be played through your web browser. Your U-PC has Firefox already installed, so you're ready to go. There are games for every interest, and all that's required is an Internet connection.

- http://www.skype.com/download/skype/linux/: How would you like to be able to speak to friends, family, coworkers, and anyone else over the Internet at no charge? Skype lets you do just that! With a broadband Internet connection (DSL or cable) and a microphone, you can speak to anyone else running the Skype application (even those running non-Linux versions) over the Internet for free! And if you have a webcam, you can let the other person see your smiling face, too. (If both parties have webcams, you have your own video-conferencing service.) Skype is a free application that installs quickly and easily on your new U-PC.

- `https://help.ubuntu.com/6.10/ubuntu/desktopguide/C/ch09s03.html`: If you're a software developer (programmer), the official Ubuntu web site has compiled a list of development tools that are compatible with Ubuntu.

- `https://help.ubuntu.com/community/AccessoriesApplications`: There are a lot of applications and tools found under Ubuntu's Application menu. My book doesn't cover them all, but this web site provides details on each and every one of them. You'll find instructions for every built-in game, as well as all the other groups: Graphics, Internet, Sound & Video, and more. Figure 12-8 shows the web page; click a group on the left side to access the page dedicated to covering that group's applications. Expect to spend some time on this site!

- `http://www.apress.com/book/view/1430219998`: I'm a fan of *Beginning Ubuntu Linux*, by Keir Thomas (from Apress). I own the third edition, but by the time you're reading this, the new fourth edition should be available. If you truly want to master all things Ubuntu, this is the book for you.

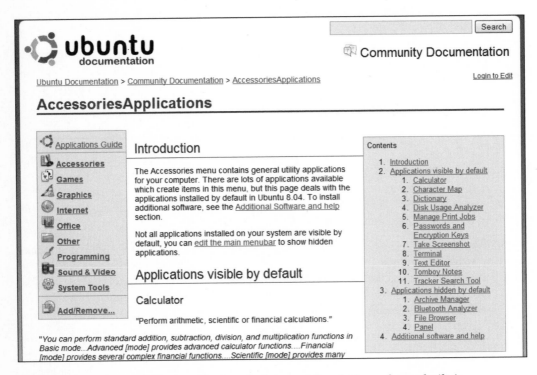

Figure 12-9. *Ubuntu's web site provides instructions and descriptions of every built-in application.*

What's Next?

The appendices. Just kidding.

You've reached the end of the book and I hope you now see just how useful, powerful, and capable the Ubuntu operating system can be. Hopefully you've also seen that Ubuntu and Ubuntu-compatible applications have a much lower demand on hardware than other operating systems. If you purchased the hardware and built your own U-PC, as described in Chapter 1, you've gone one step farther and proved that there's simply no need to go spending huge amounts of money on the latest/greatest hardware.

What's next? Spread the word. Tell your friends, family, and coworkers about your experience with Ubuntu. (And if you built your own U-PC, go ahead a brag a little, too—not many people are willing to try it, even though it's not that difficult.) Tell them how little you spent on your new computer. Then tell them how much you spent on your operating system: zero. Then tell them how much all your software set you back: zero again.

Maybe, just maybe, you'll convince a few that the days of spending $1,000, $2,000, or even more on a computer are over.

Appendix A

The U-PC that was assembled in Chapter 1 consists of a number of hardware components that were purchased on January 9, 2009. I am providing details of each component, including price, SKU, and part numbers where possible. All parts were purchased at Micro Center in Atlanta, Georgia, but can likely be found at other computer stores as well. (Micro Center also offers online shopping, so I'm including the SKU number for each part.)

Case

Description: IPSG PS TX366 Case with 300W Power Supply Unit

Micro Center SKU: 477752

Part #: None

Price: $34.99

Motherboard

Description: ECS Geforce7050M-M (2.0)

Micro Center SKU: 712778

Part #: V09204E83900970

Price: $42.99

Processor

Description: AMD Sempron 64 LE-1300

Micro Center SKU: 939413

Part #: SDH1300DPBOX

Price: $44.99

RAM Memory

Description: Crucial 1GB DDR2 PC5300

Micro Center SKU: 233973

Part #: CT12864AA667

Price: $9.99

CD/DVD Drive

Description: SAMSOEM Samsung 22x DVDRW PAT

Micro Center SKU: 933051

Part #: None

Price: $24.99

Hard Drive

Description: IPSG Western Digital 3.5" 160GB PATA HDD

Micro Center SKU: 782409

Part #: None

Price: $44.99

■**Note** All cables and connectors were included with hardware purchases at no additional cost.

Total: $202.94

Appendix B

There are three methods available for obtaining an Ubuntu installation disc. All three methods start by visiting `http://www.ubuntu.com` and clicking the Get Ubuntu link along the left side of the screen.

Method 1

Download the ISO image file and create an Ubuntu bootable disc. This will require a broadband connection to download the file (it's almost 700MB in size) and a CD/DVD-RW device to write the image to the disc. Click the "Download now" link and follow the directions to download the ISO image file.

Note Simply copying the ISO image file to the disc does not work. Creating a bootable disc from an image file requires that your CD/DVD software have the capability to write a bootable disc from an ISO file. Consult your CD/DVD authoring software documentation for assistance.

Method 2

Buy a bootable CD or DVD with the Ubuntu installation files. Visit `http://www.ubuntu.com/getubuntu` and click on the "Buy on CD or DVD" link and follow the directions to purchase a disc.

Method 3

You may also obtain a bootable Ubuntu disc for free by clicking the "Request a free CD" link and following the directions. The disc will be shipped to you at no cost, but it will take approximately 10 weeks for you to receive your free disk. (Purchasing the disc using Method 2 includes a shipping fee and provides a speedier delivery.)

APPENDIX C

■■■

Bibliography

The following list is only a jumping-off point; you're sure to find more resources to help you in your discovery of Ubuntu.

Note Some of these resources are referenced in earlier chapters.

Web Sites

`http://www.ubuntu.com`: The official Ubuntu web site and the ideal place to download the latest version and read about updates and new releases.

`http://ubuntuforums.org/`: More forums than you'll probably ever have time to visit. Be sure to check out the Absolute Beginner Talk at the top of the list—it's a great place to start if you're new to Ubuntu and have one question—or a thousand!

`www.ubuntu.com/support/communitysupport/`: One of the best web sites for help with Ubuntu.

`http://www.pcmech.com/byopc/`: If you're looking for more information on building your own PC, this is a great site to visit. You'll learn more details about the steps described in Chapter 1.

`http://ubuntuclips.org/collections_3.html`: This site contains videos that show the installation of Ubuntu as well as how to download and create the installation disc.

`http://www.getdeb.net/`: Want more free software for your U-PC? This is the place! Be sure to check out the Daily Top 10 list to see what other Ubuntu fans are downloading.

`http://en.wikipedia.org/wiki/Comparison_of_Windows_and_Linux`: This site provides a detailed comparison of Linux and Windows. Although it's not 100 percent Ubuntu-focused, the site can give you a better understanding of what Ubuntu can do.

`http://lifehacker.com/search/Ubuntu/`: Lifehacker is one of my favorite web sites and you'll find a wealth of information on Ubuntu by using this URL or just searching on "Ubuntu" at `http://lifehacker.com`.

`https://help.ubuntu.com/community/Games`: I'm not saying I play a lot of games, okay? But if you just happen to be looking for some games to play on Ubuntu (other than the ones that come preinstalled), this is a great listing of some of the best—available with links to download and install.

Books

`http://www.apress.com/book/search-searchterm=Ubuntu`: Every book that Apress publishes concerning Ubuntu. Yes, it's quite a list. This should tell you something about the success and quality of Ubuntu.

`http://www.wiley.com/WileyCDA/WileyTitle/productCd-0470125055.html`: No, you're not a dummy. Neither am I. But I own this book and it's a great resource.

`https://help.ubuntu.com/8.10/index.html`: Yes, it's a web site, but it's the Ubuntu 8.10 official documentation, and it's extremely detailed. Print out pages that you find yourself referencing often and keep them handy.

Must-Have Apps

The following are just a small sampling of some free applications that are not included with Ubuntu but should be (in this author's opinion).

`http://www.skype.com/download/skype/linux/`: Skype lets you make free "phone calls" to anyone else running the Skype application. All it requires is a high-speed Internet connection and a microphone. A webcam is optional, but it does allow video communication if both parties have webcams.

`http://www.gimp.org`: GIMP is a much more advanced photo editing application than Picasa (see Chapter 8). It's completely open source and free to download. GIMP can be a bit overwhelming to use at first, so be sure to check out some of the free tutorials hosted on the GIMP web site. If you find you need more, Apress has one of the best books available titled *Beginning GIMP, Second Edition*, by Akkana Peck.

`http://deluge-torrent.org/`: Deluge Torrent is a peer-to-peer application that will allow you to download files and share files over the Internet. Peer-to-peer apps aren't all used for illegal purposes, and you might find yourself using Deluge Torrent to download missed television shows, other free applications, and more. Not familiar with Torrent-style applications? Check out `http://www.what-is-torrent.com/` to find out more.

`http://www.adobe.com/products/flashplayer/`: Flash is a plug-in for your web browser that allows animation created using the Adobe Flash software to play onscreen. The good news is that there is a version for Ubuntu users, so you won't have to visit web sites and see a bunch of error messages about how the Flash animation won't display.

`http://www.mythtv.org/`: MythTV software allows you to turn your U-PC into a television recorder (similar to TiVo), store recorded shows on your hard drive, and watch them later. All it requires is the purchase of a TV tuner video card to your U-PC (usually around $80–$120) and a large hard drive.

Index

You Need the Companion eBook

Your purchase of this book entitles you to buy the companion PDF-version eBook for only $10. Take the weightless companion with you anywhere.

We believe this Apress title will prove so indispensable that you'll want to carry it with you everywhere, which is why we are offering the companion eBook (in PDF format) for $10 to customers who purchase this book now. Convenient and fully searchable, the PDF version of any content-rich, page-heavy Apress book makes a valuable addition to your programming library. You can easily find and copy code—or perform examples by quickly toggling between instructions and the application. Even simultaneously tackling a donut, diet soda, and complex code becomes simplified with hands-free eBooks!

Once you purchase your book, getting the $10 companion eBook is simple:

❶ Visit **www.apress.com/promo/tendollars/**.

❷ Complete a basic registration form to receive a randomly generated question about this title.

❸ Answer the question correctly in 60 seconds, and you will receive a promotional code to redeem for the $10.00 eBook.

THE EXPERT'S VOICE™

2855 TELEGRAPH AVENUE | SUITE 600 | BERKELEY, CA 94705